TO THE
ONE I LOVE
THE BEST

Also by this author

———•———

Hotel Splendide

TO THE
ONE I LOVE
THE BEST

Pushkin Press

LUDWIG
BEMELMANS

Pushkin Press
Somerset House, Strand
London WC2R 1LA

To the One I Love the Best was first published in 1955

First published by Pushkin Press in 2022

1 3 5 7 9 8 6 4 2

ISBN 13: 978-1-78227-793-4

Designed and typeset by Tetragon, London
Printed and bound by Clays Ltd, Elcograf S.p.A.

www.pushkinpress.com

TO THE
ONE I LOVE
THE BEST

Contents

———•———

PART TWO: ELSIE ABROAD

to
MOTHER
and
CHARLES
from
STEVIE
with love

PART ONE

Elsie at Home

1

Invitation

Psychologists say that an excessive intake of food and wine is a substitute for happiness. I like pudding, I like wine, roast goose, Virginia ham, shepherd's pie, and lobster stew. I am hungry and thirsty a great deal of the time, which accounts for the fact that I have acquired a reputation as a connoisseur of wines and as a gourmet. If I am hungry, then, the thing I worry about most is that one day all the goodies will be taken away from me. Oh no, not by the Russians, by someone infinitely kinder, but still taken away. I am speaking of the day or night after which a photograph of me, and a bad one, will appear on the most sombre page of the newspaper, and under it my name, and a résumé of my career, which was mainly dedicated to the enjoyment of life. At least that is what it will say, for I have also acquired a reputation as a lover of life and a professor of happiness.

I believe in God; to me He has been wonderful, kind, and generous; but I have never been able to convince myself that after I have passed through this magnificent world I'll be admitted to a place even more astonishing, to a paradise of better landscapes, restaurants, horses, dogs, cigars, and all the other objects of my adoration; for such would be my paradise. I cannot imagine myself as an angel, sitting on a cloud, forever singing, and I think it would bore the good God Himself.

For such as I, then, all is here and now, the rewards and the miracles. They are the green tree, the sunrise, and all the things we sing about—the jet plane, the paintbrush and the easel, the cadets of West Point, and especially children, most of all babies with their grave, observant eyes.

In spite of all that the black moods descend upon me, and consolation is hard to find. I can't be helped by psychiatrists, for, of those I know, several have committed suicide, a dozen have been divorced, and the best of them have the look of the haunted and bewildered or radiate the false effusiveness of the overstimulated. I lie on my own couch, suspended in cosmic gloom, the eye turned inward, and it takes me a while to console myself.

There are two cures. One is to work; all misery fades when I work, but I can't work all the time. The other is to celebrate. I, the confirmed lover of life and professor of happiness, look as we all must at life, and at the approaching day when we can only hope to be mourned for. I get hungry again and have to hurry and reassure myself with another good bottle and a fine meal, and after the coffee I look through the blue smoke of my good cigar. I sit in the melancholy mood that is like cello music and search for the answers we shall never know.

People such as I live by rules of their own. We are not happy with the comforts that the group offers. We are off-horses, misfits, we don't fit into the classes. We are not of the labouring class, the professional type, the manufacturer or salesman group, not even of that indigent company that collects in low bars or the brotherhood of the flophouses. In the design that has been imposed upon humanity we are solitary, self-appointed outcasts. Outcast is too dramatic a word; let's call us alone goers. That also is not quite true, for I seek people and like them, but still in their midst I am alone.

My life has been coloured mostly by a period spent in the army, as a medic in the violent wards of an insane hospital. I learned there to block myself against things, to impose a rigid discipline on my own mind and emotions. And to be equally impersonal with the patients, for otherwise I could never have been of help to them. I learned there also to regard death as a generous manifestation, and to love life all the more for this discovery. And for the good of the soul I learned to step outside of myself, to forget the 'I', which is the key to happiness.

Another detail of my character is that I am contrary by nature and I always take the other side. Also I hate to order roundtrip tickets; I go one way, because I hold before me the possibility that I may never come back. A nonconformer, then, I came to Hollywood, and decided again to be contrary. At that time they gave money away, and I received a heap of it for the original stories they bought from me, and also a contract that gave me more than I could ever have hoped for in the wildest calculations. I've always been careless with money; it seemed illogical to me to save any of it when there wasn't much anyway.

Now there was, and it seemed to make sense to be miserly. I had rented a little cabin, a shack at the beach in Topango, for forty dollars a month. I always go the whole hog. I decided I'd wash my own socks, sweep up and make my bed, shine my shoes, and work. I wanted to paint. The money I had, and the money I would save, would allow me to do what I wanted for the rest of my life—that is, be an itinerant painter travelling across America in my little car and painting the country. I had bought a second-hand Ford convertible, and with this I would commute to the studio. The elegant world of Hollywood, the life of the stars, all that was to be left to one side.

The studio had engaged a suite for me at the Beverly Hills Hotel. I stayed there until I bought the car and found the shack. When I went back to the hotel for the last time, to pick up my mail and my belongings before driving out to the beach, there were many invitations, among them one to come to cocktails at Lady Mendl's. I had heard of her. She was a very old lady and a decorator, and she interested me. She was outside the things I had marked as off-limits. I accepted this one invitation. I'm very glad I did, for since I met her, when I sit and look through the blue haze of my cigar, there always appears the one creature who gave me inspiration, who fought the phantoms, who, day in and out, set me an example that made beautiful sense.

She weighed about ninety pounds without her jewels, and when I met her she was ninety years old.

When you live here and there and travel a lot, the seasons run into each other, and the years lose shape, especially if part of the time is spent in Hollywood.

The war was almost over; I had worked with the OWI and finished a guide for the troops in France. I had written the story for an anti-Nazi film called *The Blue Danube* and for another called *Yolanda and the Thief*. There were plans for producing both of these. There were the usual meetings with the agent and the producer. I was quartered in an office, elegant and air-conditioned, and, as I have said, I got the old car and drove to the Beverly Hills Hotel to move to the beach, and there was, among others, the message which said: 'While you were out, Lady Mendl's secretary, Miss West, called to ask you for cocktails tomorrow around six.'

I experience an occasional pleasant illusion. It is the dreamlike sensation that in a former existence I was a person of great consequence, one who lived in marble halls, a munificent, benevolent king, marquis, or a prince. (All other people who share this belief find that they were equally well placed; no one has ever told me that in a former life he was a butler, a dishwasher, or a policeman.) In consequence of this, I have a great preference for palaces, magnificent interiors, for faded silvered mirrors, marbles, and antique statuary.

In Hollywood one can find almost anything; but I did not expect to find there the reincarnation of the scenes of a former life and to come across a little palace exactly like the lovely silver and blue Amalienburg that stands in the park of Nymphenburg outside Munich. Nor hope to find therein, reflected in faded mirrors, the fabulous creature who with discipline unmatched defied the eternal fears.

2

The Footstool of Madame Pompadour

Because nobody walks in Hollywood, we are now driving along Benedict Canyon Drive in Beverly Hills, looking for a place called 'After All'. The number of the house is 1018. In this latitude it would be too much to expect that a house whose interior is baroque would have an exterior to match. So 1018 is California Spanish on the outside. In front is a large sanded place to park—it looks as if a party were taking place, about a dozen cars are parked close to the house. We drive around a circular patch of carefully tended grass, from the precise centre of which rises the trunk of a tall eucalyptus tree. These trees ordinarily are sloppy, their bark hangs in shreds, like an overcoat about to be cast off. This one is meticulously groomed.

Under the tree is a green garden table, and at the table with a file cabinet sits a woman of ample proportions. She looks up and smiles, she has emerald-coloured eyes, and, as she gets up, half a dozen kittens fall from her lap.

'Those are my puthy cats and kitty cats,' she says, 'and without them I don't know what I would do. And you are

Mr Bemelmans. Welcome to After All. I am Lady Mendl's secretary—my name is Hilda West.'

The arriving guest is protected against the California dew by a porte-cochère with green-and-white-striped canvas storm curtains. Through a green foyer we enter the house and turn right to go into the salon. The interior is like that of the castle in Nymphenburg (the illusion of the former existence presents itself for a moment). The room is empty, there is no party, the cars belong to Lady Mendl's hairdresser, to Dr Hauser, to the manicurist, to Sir Charles Mendl, to the florist, and to a very special electrician by the name of Mr Nightingale, who tells me all this while he is busy lighting a small menagerie of crystal animals in a glass cabinet.

The butler approaches with tremendous aplomb and says, 'Lady Mendl will be with you in a minute.'

Even if we only know a person from what we read and hear, we form a definite opinion. In my mind I had designed Lady Mendl exactly as she was.

There are statues of saints in Latin countries, especially in Spain, the most beautiful in Seville, that are carried about the city at night during Holy Week. They move a little stiffly on floats, borne on the backs of penitents, and in the lights of hundreds of candles. They are loaded with jewels, in silver robes; they have flowers of silver in their hair; men with silver trumpets precede them, and the Spanish increase the mortification of the penitents by throwing glowing cigar and cigarette butts in their path. The penitents curse, and the statues in the flickering lights seem to show as much commiseration as Spanish etiquette permits.

As she came towards me this mood of things Spanish and churchly was in the room, but only for the eye and the moment, for as she advanced farther she changed completely. She had on a severe black dress made by Mainbocher, with a gold fob at the side as the only decoration. Her legs were like those of a little girl, and well shod, in low-heeled black shoes that a ballerina might wear. She pulled the skirt away at the sides and straightened it out, and then stuck her gloved hands in two pockets and with her chin motioned to a white couch on which were three pillows, in deep sea-green satin with letters embroidered in white silk.

The first pillow read: 'It takes a stout heart to live without roots.' On the second was: 'Never explain, never complain.' And on the third: 'Who rides a tiger can never descend.' We sat down. On the right was an onyx fireplace, and on the mantel stood an exquisite small coral-red clock, the only object in this room not white, silver, or green. We faced a vast mirror, oxidized, and fogged with age.

She looked at me in this mirror (most of our conversations took place via this mirror) and after the get-acquainted talk she said, 'Stevie, I have very clear eyes. I have second sight and instant recognition. We will be very good friends, you and I, such good friends that when Mother talks to you it will be as if she talked to herself.'

She leaned against me, took my arm and my hand, and went on looking into the mirror as she said, 'Mother has invented a cocktail, made of gin and grapefruit juice and cointreau. It sounds revolting, but try it, you may like it, but if you don't, just tell Mother, and you can have anything else you want. Never take anything you don't want. I'm a wanter, and so are you—I know you very well. You and I, we live by the eye, and that's why we are friends.'

The butler passed a tray with the Lady Mendl cocktails on it. She watched my face in the mirror as I tasted it, and she said to the butler, 'Take it away and bring him a scotch and soda'—which was precisely what I wanted.

'But you like this room, Stevie? There is nothing in it that offends you?'

I don't know why she called me Stevie, probably because a war was going on with Germany and she didn't like the Teutonic 'Ludwig'.

'Stevie, listen to Mother. I was born in an ugly house, in an ugly street, the last of five children. I was told that I was ugly by my parents, by both of them, and the furniture in that house was ugly too, and I always got the dark meat of the chicken. I made myself like it, the dark meat, but that's the only thing I compromised on. "For the rest," I said, looking into that very clear, cruel mirror in my room, "if I am ugly, and I am, I am going to make everything around me beautiful. That will be my life. To create beauty! And my friends will be those who create beauty"—and I have held to that every day of my life. I said to myself, like Dr Coué advised people to say to themselves, "Every day I am feeling better and better"—so I said, every day, "I will make my small niche in the world more and more beautiful." And beautiful things are faithful friends, and they stay beautiful, they become more beautiful as they get older—my lovely house, my lovely garden. I could steal for beauty, I could kill for it.'

A new transformation had been going on. She now had the sharp profile of Voltaire. She kicked me in the ribs with her elbow and cried, '*Ha!* Vulgarity marches on like a plague, and everything is getting cold and ugly.'

The butler passed with cocktail food.

'Is it cold out, Coombs?'

'Not really cold, milady, but I'd say fur-coat cold.'

'Mother is free tonight, Stevie. Would you take her to dinner? I eat very frugally and I hardly drink.'

A maid brought in a very carefully groomed miniature poodle.

'This is Mr Bemelmans,' said Mother, introducing me to the dog, 'one of the family. And this is Blue Blue.'

Blue Blue had no interest in me; he sat down and stared, immobile as a chameleon in a tree. Mother said, 'Dear Blue Blue! He went and bit the wheels of the locomotive, the last time we left Paris—he knew how I hated to leave. I have a house in Versailles, the Villa Trianon, and I was almost done decorating it when the Germans came.

'Speaking of the villa, only yesterday a little souvenir arrived from there, a little part of its glory—a footstool that once belonged to Pompadour. There it is, Stevie, please move it over—there's a little patch of sunlight in the centre of the room. Place it there so we can properly appreciate it.'

I moved the delicate piece of furniture into the sunlight.

'It's been in storage, it's been lonesome and cold. Mother feels about that, for she has hung her heart on objects like that—and there are so many more locked up and in hiding, and I must go and get them out and finish the villa. But you know, Stevie'—and now I got the second kick in the ribs—'I am a self-made woman, and everything you see here I have bought with my own money, but somehow there is never enough. I never, never have enough money to buy all the beautiful things that I want in this world, and to do all the things I want to do. But never mind that; I always manage. Now let's look at the footstool.'

The sun had moved from it, and I had to place it anew. It was mounted on four emerald-coloured legs with golden claws. A row of silver nails in the shape of fleurs-de-lis held down a petit-point cover that was as delicate as the illuminations on medieval manuscripts.

There was the sound of a car outside, and then the door opened. There entered life, in the person of Sir Charles Mendl. He came towards us and smiled with a jolly face that was like a ripe plum lying a little on its side. The plum was festooned with a Colonel Blimp moustache.

'This is my dear husband—' Mother started to say.

As Sir Charles extended his hand he tripped over Madame Pompadour's footstool and lay on the floor, very still.

'My God, he's dead,' said Lady Mendl.

'Nonsense,' answered Sir Charles. 'I'm not dead. Having played polo all my life, I simply know how to fall. When one falls one remains absolutely still for a minute. Now don't anyone bother helping me up.'

He remained quiet for what seemed a long time.

'Are you resting, dear?' asked Lady Mendl.

'Yes, I'm resting,' said Sir Charles.

'Well, don't overdo it.'

Sir Charles was watching the dial on his wristwatch. At the end of a minute he got up.

Mother put one fist to her hip and stamped her foot. She slapped me on the back hard and said, 'You search the world for beauty, for beautiful things to live with; you fill your home with the most exquisite pieces and you place them right; all is perfect, and then in comes your husband wearing that awful coat—that inseparable, impermeable, confounded trench coat—and ruins all the effect so carefully established.'

Ignoring these words, his plum face leaning back so that he spoke to the ceiling rather than to us, Sir Charles answered, 'This coat was given me on the occasion of my visit to the Maginot Line. The Maginot Line, being French, did not keep out the Germans; but this coat, being British, I daresay, still keeps out the rain—and I shall keep on wearing it. I am as fond of it as you are of your precious antiques, my dear.'

The butler had taken the offending garment and also the footstool, and Lady Mendl, with a curious smile in which she lifted her upper lip and showed her teeth, said, 'This is my dear husband, Sir Charles Mendl.' The hand was extended a second time, and she added, 'Dear Charles, do me a favour—go out and come in again. I love to see you come into this house without that coat.' Sir Charles obliged.

Sir Charles had a late paper, and the headline was about Paris.

'Oh, to think that France is free again!' said Mother with a saintly face, clasping the white-gloved hands. 'Dear Paris, dear Versailles! I shall see my villa again!'

'Dear Paris,' said Sir Charles, 'and the French—awfully depressing, especially if you speak the language.'

'There are a few things Charles and I don't agree on. They are diet, the French, and beautiful things. For example, this poor dear footstool of Madame Pompadour's. It could have been in this house a hundred years, and if he hadn't fallen over it, dear Charles would never have been aware of its presence.'

Lady Mendl then asked him, 'I wonder how soon one can fly to Paris?'

Sir Charles was seated. Glancing at his paper, he said, 'A plane crashed—fifty people killed.'

'Anyone we know, Charles dear?'

'No, Elsie, it was a Canadian plane.'

'I know some Canadians, very nice people,' said Elsie.

Charles said he hoped that none of them were on board that plane, and then he excused himself and went to his room.

'Dear Charles,' said Elsie, 'he's such a snob. You know, he has a pain in his right leg, and he insists that it's the same disease that the King has.' She leaned over and said in confidence, 'He's getting a little gaga, poor dear. He's taking on the prerogatives of children, like running off to his room to sulk. But it's refreshing to have a husband who is still attractive to women and who behaves properly. With all the nonsense going on here, it gives me great pleasure. You know how it is with anyone out here who has a title and is an international figure! He has been to see the Pope in private audience, he's received all the ambassadors and distinguished people, he is superb at arranging seatings at table, and he looks so wonderful against the fireplace. Of course the dear man knows nothing about furniture or beautiful things; he makes faces when he has to look at paintings at an exhibition.'

Charles came back into the room. Looking at me, he asked, 'I say, where are the oysters better, at Romanoff's or at La Rue?'

I said they were best at Chasen's, because there was a much larger turnover.

Elsie looked at him sharply. 'Charles, who are you dining with?'

'Oh, a very ravishing creature.'

'Is it as mysterious as all that?'

'No, Elsie dear, but I can't recall. I have to look in my little book.'

He wandered off to his room again, and I received the third poke.

'You see what I mean,' said Elsie in a deep voice and with the Voltaire face. 'Charles is getting old—he can't remember any more.'

He came back with the pince-nez on his nose and his little black book open. 'I'm not dining out. I'm dining in, with Joan Fontaine, at her house.'

'Is she a good cook?'

'I don't know her that well,' said Charles and left again.

'Mother is going upstairs for a minute, and then we'll take the car. And may Mother bring a friend—Blue Blue? And where are we going to dine, Stevie?'

'At Romanoff's,' I said.

Mother clicked her tongue and made a few faces of youthful anticipation and stamped her feet.

Sir Charles appeared once more. 'I'll be back rather late, dear. I'm taking Joan to a concert after dinner. Heifetz is playing.'

Mother took a stance again, stuck her hands in her pockets and smiled, and left to go upstairs. Later, in the car, she said, 'Oh, those musical evenings! Dear Charles is musical. He sings. They say he has a good voice—he has volume and sings notes within notes. As for Heifetz, they say he is the best, but when I come out of one of his concerts I don't know whether I have been to it or not. It isn't music to me. I could just as well have watched him wind a clock.'

'Here is Romanoff's—*chk*—I like Mr Romanoff very much. He welcomes dogs in his restaurant.'

We had a good, slow, quiet dinner, and two bottles of wine. There was some talking, but also the long silences that usually come only after long acquaintance and friendship. When I said good night to Mother at the door of her house I promised to come back the next day for lunch.

I found that I was happy to be with her. She was as comprehensible to me as if I had painted her a dozen times. She was uncomplicated, she was ageless. I observed her closely and at first with some fear that the perfection of this wonderful living objet d'art might have flaws, but I found out that it was perfect, and for me it stayed so. I looked sharply at her in the first days. Just as she covered up her crêpy throat with jewels and her arthritic hands with gloves, so she covered or ignored those things in life that age other people. Her will to live happily, or at least beautifully, was so formidable that it triumphed over nature itself. She was younger than all the starlets, she had reckless courage, the gift of friendship, and a restless, enquiring mind.

In the stages of life that were behind her, Elsie Lady Mendl had graduated from an ugly child to a young woman who became a mediocre actress. Of the photographs of her and the paintings, during the years that followed, one would say, to be kind, that she appeared to be a nice enough person but without any distinction. She had no children, she never spoke of her family. Yet now she was beautiful; at the height of life she had achieved a shining quality.

Her face had the luminous pallor of a porcelain statue, young and alert. She had invented the bluing of hair and wore ribbons, jewels, or golden leaves in hers. She exercised hard and adhered to a rigid diet prescribed for her by Dr Hauser. She followed all his advice with the exception of blackstrap molasses, and this I think she refused because she hated black, and any other mournful shade, in all objects with the exception of motor cars and black dresses.

After her ordinary morning exercises she devoted a daily half-hour to her eyes, exercising them by various routines and by flitting sunlight into them through a large magnifying glass. As a result she had the vision of a bird of prey. She was self-made, she was American. She spoke a schoolgirl French and in English she pronounced furniture 'foiniture' and servants 'soivants'.

She insisted on perfection in the running of her house and she had a passion for beautiful things—and these qualities lent her such strength that those who came near her gladly submitted to the discipline she inflicted on herself. All the bums of Hollywood got off their high-wheeled bicycles and behaved themselves, and the most vulgar women turned gentle in her presence.

In Hollywood at that time everyone's bread was thickly buttered; the restaurants were filled and people stood waiting in lines. All things were intensely purposeful, and the streets and stages were crowded with eager people, all of whom acted one thing while they rehearsed another. Life ran at the speed of a newsreel.

'Only I trail the chiffons of time,' Mother said—which was not true. When I tried to adjust myself to her tempo I found that I had to hurry.

My departure from the hotel was put off, for there were always invitations. In the many gradations of friendship, this one ripened fast. 'When you are as old as Mother you know who you are with; you see very clearly and instantly, and everything is right.'

One day when I came to the house West said, 'Well, you are one of the family now. I can always tell. Mother listens only to nice things, you will observe, and when she is very happy she makes a face like a little girl in a new dress; she radiates. When I say that a big bouquet of white lilies has arrived from Mr Cukor, or when I announce that Mr Litvak has sent a Chinese silk rug, she smiles happily; and she also smiles happily when I say that you have accepted for lunch or dinner. Although you haven't sent flowers or a rug, Mother loves you.'

This revelation brought me great happiness. I went immediately to the best florist and sent Mother a bouquet of his finest white roses.

3

At Home

Soon after, at Elsie's invitation, I moved into a little apartment at After All, the most comfortable place I have ever known. It consisted of a bedroom, a small study, a dressing room, and a bath.

Mother had said, 'Come in and consider this your house.' And then she had taken me upstairs and said, 'Now, look, Stevie, this is your room, all for yourself, with air-conditioning. You can make it as warm as you like, or as cold, by flicking this switch. Put the dial at the desired temperature and it will stay that way.

'The windows are fixed so that you can have it pitch-dark at high noon. Here is your dressing room, and Miss Bridget will put your things away after Coombs unpacks you. Here are places for your shoes and for your hats and shirts and ties—I copied this room in miniature from a haberdasher's shop in London. You don't have to bend down for anything. It's all there, at your hand. Here is a closet where you put the things you're not always using, like raincoats. This is the bathroom—'

It took a while to know that it was the bathroom. The bath was behind a curtain. The tub had a bridge across it, with a shaving mirror; a rack for magazines was within reach; there were also a submersible pillow and a headrest. Behind a door were what Elsie called the 'unspeakable' and a washbasin, and there were cupboards for towels and toilet articles. The room itself had a daybed and a desk.

'This is altogether yours. For anything you want, you have Coombs. You do just as you please. Come and go when you want to. You don't even have to talk to us when you don't feel like it. Just let Coombs know that you'll be out for dinner, or in. And if these terrible people don't take care of you, you tell Mother, and Mother will get after them.'

I would spend most of the day at the shack on the beach, working, and come home towards five. After dressing, I went down and waited for Elsie. She inspected her menageries and paintings and put everything in order, and then she sat down close to me, and via the faded mirror told me her credo as a decorator.

'Are you happy here, Stevie?'

'Yes, very, Mother.'

'And you have everything you want?'

'Yes, it's perfect.'

'And do you like your room?'

'I have never been happier about a room.'

'And the bathroom?'

'The bathroom is the first I have seen that I like.'

'I don't know how long people have lived in houses and used furniture. I suppose you would call that time the beginning of civilization—the time they first sat on a chair instead of on the floor. Well, in all this time, and with people like Norman Bel Geddes and Raymond Loewy and Frank Lloyd Wright around, nobody with the exception of Mother has designed a bathroom that you don't have to blush when you walk into it. That monstrosity—the unspeakable porcelain fixture—even I haven't been able to defeat it. I have hidden it in a Louis Fourteenth cane chair in that closet next to your bathroom— and that's no solution either.

'They call everything they design functional. Well, that thing is certainly functional. You know, if anyone designed a decent-looking bathtub and a decent-looking unspeakable, he would be terribly rich overnight. And those things that the French call *la vase de nuit* ask for improvement also. If all these functional designers can't solve the problem, it would almost be better to go back to the outdoor plumbing of our fathers. That, at least, wasn't part of the house.

'It can be done. Stevie, remember what Mother tells you: the most important things in designing furniture—or any-thing we use—are the three genies of the fairy whose name is Good Taste, and they're called *"Simplicity"*, *"Suitability"*, and *"Proportion"*. And that goes for the bathroom as well as the salon. But let's come out of the bathroom. Did you by any chance look at the album of photographs of Versailles that Mother put on your desk?

'Well, when I speak of Versailles—and I will almost every day, for it is my life, and a perfect thing—you must not think of the Château de Versailles, for that is an ugly, vulgar pile of which the builders and occupants themselves got so tired that they went elsewhere whenever they could. When I speak of Versailles, the perfect house, which is never immense, which is never vulgar, and which is never a collection of ballrooms with cubbies for sleeping squeezed in between.

'My villa is like those retreats that women who loved houses and furniture built for themselves. The first one that came to my notice was a place called La Grotta, a little studio apartment of Isabella d'Este, the Marchioness of Mantua—small, reticent, simple, and built back around 1490. Twenty years later she established the Paradiso, an apartment she occupied after her husband's death. There was another woman who took a stand, the Marquise de Rambouillet. She resigned from the hurly-burly of court life and built herself an exquisite intimate retreat. That was when the Medici were in France and the court was like café society today.

'The most important thing to a woman, be she queen or peasant, is the house. In a house you are born, and most people die there, and the most important thing in the house is the woman, and she usually calls it "her" house. Yet, when you study the plans of architects, even the best of them, for small houses, you see that the woman is completely forgotten. She is allowed in the kitchen, in the dining-room, in the awful bathroom, and in what is called the master's bedroom. The children have a playroom, the car has a garage, the husband has a study, even the dog has a place to himself. The woman has nothing—no privacy whatever. Not a single house except those of the very advanced has a place set aside—and I don't mean a boudoir—a place of her own for the woman to retreat to.

'Well, I thought about that a lot,' Mother said in her deepest voice, 'and I did something about it. I took the bull by the horns and made a liveable house—and you don't have to have millions to do it. Oh, my dear little first house—it is still standing. We'll go and take a look at it when we are in New York again.'

A little clock went ding-ding-ding, and another answered with a higher ring, as if a very fine glass was being clinked with a fingernail.

'My darling clocks,' said Elsie. 'Someday I shall tell you about clocks. Oh, the clocks of the old days—that was something to fight, too. They had clocks that told the time and nothing else. Now, I don't particularly care if the clock isn't exactly right, or even if it stands still altogether, as long as it is beautiful. Look at that darling little red clock over there. It is made of the costliest materials, by Fabergé. All that great artist's skill is evident in it. It has proportion, suitability, and simplicity. It cost a fortune and it's never kept the right time, but Mother loves it. Besides, there is always someone to tell you what time it is. Coombs, what is the right time?'

The butler looked at his wristwatch and said, 'We're approaching cocktails, milady.'

'There was a time,' Mother went on, 'when butlers didn't wear wristwatches while on duty, or any other kind of jewellery, except a wedding ring; and some wore those even if they were not married, to give themselves an air of respectability and get a family man's excuses for extra time off.

'But that's enough for today,' said Mother. 'I hope I haven't bored you. And here comes Atwater Kent. He also has the right time. He owns a factory that makes wristwatches, among other things.'

Mr Kent was a little sharp-eyed man, small and quick. He loved to give money away outside of business hours and he was extremely hospitable. At least once a week he stood at the entrance to his vast living-room, receiving his guests and anyone they brought along, which enlarged his parties to many times the size he had planned. This mass visitation became quite a strain on him, and his guests took advantage of the wear and tear. Clifton Webb, for example, instead of saying, 'Good evening,' would say, 'I just killed my mother,' and Mr Kent would politely answer, 'How charming of you to come.'

Coombs got the card table ready, and Mr Kent, who could afford it, proceeded to lose the sixteen or eighteen dollars that Mother won from him every afternoon.

4

Benedict Canyon

'When I first came here, I regularly was stopped by the police for walking. It's not against the law to take a stroll, but it's not done much, and makes you a suspicious character. Now the police know me and I'm not bothered.'

I was walking uphill on Benedict Canyon with Sir Charles. He walked every evening.

He stopped and looked around and then he said, 'May I ask you a very great favour? There is no one out, no one to see this, but would you, dear boy, bend down and tie my shoelace? It's gotten loose and I can't bend down that low.' I tied his shoelace. 'I'm so very grateful to you.' We walked on.

'My manservant, John, is pure gold. That is, he was pure gold, now he's just gold—since he married. He took as wife an American woman, and she insists that he take a day off, and on that day I am helpless. I can't ask that butler of Elsie's to come and do anything, or the chauffeur; they are her servants and in league against anyone else. You will feel that if you haven't already. This ridiculous Coombs, now—that's not his name at all. His name is Colombe and he's French. But Elsie has a penchant for changing names, and just as she changed you from Ludwig to Stevie, she changed Colombe to Coombs. She has a maid whose name was Juliet; she changed that to Bridget.

'"Miss Bridget", as she calls her, is Australian, and is the best of all housemaids, but she is independent, as Colonials are apt to be. That causes friction. Then there is another man about whom I must warn you, not a servant—he's what I call a housefly, a Frenchman by name of La Flèche. Elsie calls him "The Golden Arrow". He suffers from illusions of grandeur. He is part decorator, part landscape architect. He is a walking encyclopaedia on these things, a reincarnation of Le Nôtre, who built a great deal of Paris. That is what Elsie says he is. They sit together and plan things, new houses, new gardens… Elsie alone is bad enough, but when he is with her, it is as if you fed hashish to a maniac—she goes up like a firework—and the consequences are always awful.

'She is a remarkable woman, utterly selfish and at the same time irresponsibly generous. She is incapable of adjustment to the life of our day. She is perhaps the incarnation of some-one—I don't know, however, of whom, for no one like her has ever lived or will come after her.

'La Flèche is happy here. He has a job building a castle or a villa a day for a motion-picture company. He's in Palm Springs, building the Taj Mahal for Zanuck. His only disappointment is that these things stand but a few days. He too dreams of Versailles.

'The other day there was a picture of Elsie in the *Hobo News*, and it said that she was a hundred. Well, she hasn't far to go, and I hope she will reach it—if for no other reason, just to give a party. Elsie loves nothing so much as a party. As to her age, she was presented at court when Queen Victoria was in her prime. Maybe she's a hundred. Her passport says that she is ninety.

'Elsie claims she is psychic and that she can feel people. She says of people that they have an aura about them, or not. Those that have the aura become her immediate friends; you, dear boy, have that aura; so has Coombs, so has Achille, the chauffeur. They, of course, have servants' auras—a small halo. I'm afraid I have none whatever.

'As her generosity is limitless, so is her avarice. She is capable of a shopkeeper's penny-pinching. One day, in sheer caprice, she had an electric meter installed so that the electricity I used could be tabulated, and presented me with a bill for the current used in my part of the house. A week later, on my birthday, she presented me with a pair of cufflinks that cost several thousand.

'It was all right to live like that, in the grand manner, years ago. But now one can't get any money out of England, the taxes are frightful, the cost of living is out of all bounds; but of none of that does Elsie take account. I have a hard time to keep up my end of it, but it's not enough, and poor Elsie is continually in trouble to make ends meet. She overpays the servants, hands out tips like a *nouveau riche*, buys things she cannot afford—at a time when there are millionaires whose wives do their own housework. She turns psychic when you talk to her about it, and she will tell you that she has a recurrent dream that would come true if she was ever in real difficulty. The dream is a typical Elsie dream. It takes place in the château at Versailles. A fat man, carrying two sacks, enters the villa. The sacks, of course, are filled with bullion, and the entire salon is filled with the light of that gold as he pours it on the table—a very expensive Louis Fourteenth table, of course, and the man naturally resembles Louis Fourteenth, her favourite Louis.

'I, on the other hand, am not psychic. I dream of realities, and they are tonight, as on most other nights, awful nightmares, and in them, larger than all the other dark objects, looms the shadow of the villa at Versailles. It was an old house when she got it; it was always in need of repairs. It was draughty, and there was no joy in it for me. At the time, however, I had my own *garçonnière* in Paris, where I could live by myself when I wanted to get away. That's very important, dear boy—to have a place to be alone. In Elsie's houses there is no room for anyone who has need of privacy. I think you are very wise to have rented that little place—a shack, anything—to get away, especially if you must do some work.

'I've been thinking of rounding out my income. Zanuck has promised me a part in a picture, and a Mr Halvah, who is very important as an agent, has told me that any time I wished to he'd arrange for me to give a concert. Perhaps a series of them. He has even spoken of a spot on the radio. Now, that would be ideal. I don't know if I have told you, but I have a fairly good voice.

'Now, are you properly taken care of? Are your boots and clothes looked after well? I needn't ask that. Since you have an aura, naturally Elsie has given orders.' Sir Charles stopped, then said, 'I think we had better turn around now and go back.

'Another thing,' he continued. 'Elsie judges everything by houses and people by their furniture. I know some awfully nice people that have terrible furniture and houses. There is a man here, awfully nice chap, by name of Munchin. I've tried to bring him to the house, but Elsie won't have him. Owns everything under the sun, so rich that he has the greatest legal talent handling his tax problems. Still Elsie won't have him. On the other hand—you will see for yourself tonight—we're going to the house of a man who is a perfect rotter. Name is Ringelnatz—he controls a good deal of the entertainment business—and he's giving a Halloween party. For the entertainment he has a circus, and because he asked Elsie to give him ideas for the decorations she is entranced with him.

'So tonight you will find yourself sitting in a huge tent which is, naturally, striped, white and green—green is Elsie's favourite colour. Striped green is her delight. She will be the Queen of Halloween. When one goes to a house like that, where they have Negro butlers who are always drunk and laughing, and where last year someone was found drowned in the pool, one is cautious. I have asked for the table—who is at it?—now here it is.' Sir Charles pulled out a piece of paper. 'Elsie is at the right of Mr Ringelnatz, you are on her right, next to you is a Miss Nordholm, a ravishing creature, Swedish and very talented. Next to her is—that agent, Mr Halvah, who is known locally as the Thief of Baghdad, Turkish Delight. And people say also that Halvah is a four-letter word. He's a very bad hat. For the rest, you have some nice people—if a bit dull.'

Going downhill was easier than up. As we came back to the house Achille was dusting my car.

'See what I mean, he's not allowed to touch mine… We have half an hour to change now. We don't dress usually. Dark suit is good enough. But tonight the old girl expects us to be in the salon at six-thirty, dressed.'

5

The Snake Charmer

The little red clock struck quarter to six as I walked into the salon. The candles were not lit; the room was in twilight. I went to the farthest corner of the room and sat down near the fireplace. The fire wasn't lit either. The butler and the footmen were busy carrying in a huge armchair, and Sir Charles, who directed the operation, looked around and finally said, 'Place it here, Coombs, near this lamp. I like to sit here and read and look out into the garden.' They put the armchair in place.

Sir Charles looked at it and asked them to turn it a little. 'That's perfect,' he said.

Coombs placed his hands on the backrest of the easy chair. 'Beg pardon, sir, but don't you think, sir, that this chair would be happier in your room, sir?'

'If I thought so, Coombs, I would have asked you to take it there.'

'Very well, sir, as you wish, sir.'

Charles left, and Coombs folded his hands over his chest and looked at the chair, and the footman matched the butler's face and then also folded his hands in the same fashion.

'Wait till she sees this chair,' said Coombs.

I had become accustomed to the light and I saw that the armchair they had brought in was something like a pullman chair, a vast piece of furniture, a *meuble* that accommodated itself to the contours of the body. It could be lengthened into a chaise longue, and the piece that supported the legs had a mechanism which could be raised so that the legs were in their most relaxed position, the knees up, the feet at the level of the stomach. The butler and the footman pulled it into several positions. It was like an upholstered operating table; it was covered in light green leather, and the leather was attached to the wood with white upholsterer's tacks.

'I would take it to Sir Charles's room just before she comes down,' said the assistant.

Both men again looked at the chair.

'Yes, Mr Coombs, I would take a chance and put it in Sir Charles's room.'

'If I did that he'd cut my throat.'

'And if you leave it here?'

'She'll cut my throat.'

'Well, I see where you'll have two cut throats then, and besides, she may cut you out of her will as well. This is serious.'

'Oh, I'm not worried about that. You know Mother. She's not going to leave anybody anything anyway. She's going to leave all her money to a dog, and it won't be Sir Charles—it will be Blue Blue. He will have the house and servants and he'll send out invitations: "Mr Blue Blue requests the pleasure, etc." Eventually the place will go to a dog pound. Can't you see Sir Charles on his knees forcing cod-liver oil down Blue Blue's throat?'

The little clock which did not keep the right time sounded six o'clock with silvery ping-ping-ping-ping-ping-ping. 'Let's hurry,' said Coombs, 'she'll be down any minute.' They ran out of the room as West came in. I stood up.

West followed the butler and the footman with her eyes. 'Oh, how I hate that butler!' she said. 'I'd laugh if I ever saw him floating past me dead. I'd like to cut off his ears and his nose and his moustache and then kick his teeth in. He gets the highest wages and does nothing for it. Look at the time. The room is dark, and the fire isn't lit.'

The butler and the footman came in with matches. They ran to light the candles and the fire.

Coombs then took up a position near the stairs. He looked like a cross between Clifton Webb and an old horse that was tired in the flanks. He had Webb's debonair disdain in his upturned face, that same mouth and a toothbrush kind of moustache, the colour of manila rope, and similar eyebrows, usually raised half-way up his forehead, and the same colour hair. The body was caved in at the shoulders, the chest, the back, and the abdomen; it was like a broken crate with cloth draped over it. He looked English rather than French, and he moved about with very important gestures, stooped forward with his bony hands on the lapels of his coat or folded over his chest or in back of him. He had about six set positions, like a soldier's manual of arms. He had another mechanism for carrying trays and serving food. His general behaviour changed according to the people in the room. When he was in a room with Sir Charles he was formal. With Sir Charles and Lady Mendl he was cautious and reserved and always on the side of the room where she stood. When there were additional people he became aloof. When he was alone he was a sad old horse, and in West's presence he became hostile. He now stood respectfully still, looking up to the first-floor landing, and then he dropped his hands and leaped up the stairs, in case Lady Mendl wanted him to help her descend.

'Good evening, milady,' he said. 'What a lovely dress milady is wearing tonight.'

'Thank you, Coombs.'

'When does milady wish the car?'

'We're going to a party right after cocktails, Coombs.'

Achille, the chauffeur, was in the doorway. Coombs turned to him. 'The car in about an hour, Achille, and you have the address.'

'Yes, I got the address,' said Achille.

Elsie suddenly stopped and stared at the chair. 'What's that?' she said.

'That's a nice chair, milady,' said Achille.

'Well, I'm glad you like it,' said Elsie. 'I give it to you under condition that you take it out of here and home immediately.'

The chair shone like a newly polished shoe.

'What's this chair doing in this house?' Elsie asked in terrible tones.

'It was given me,' said Charles, who had just emerged from the corridor that led to his room. 'It was given me by Mr Munchin, the man I spoke to you about, Elsie, the one who owns so many things and, among them, the factory that makes these chairs. Try it. It's the ultimate in comfort.'

Elsie turned to the butler and sent him on an errand. He was unhappy to leave and looked back, like a little boy sent out of the room while the older one is being spanked.

'It's your favourite colour, the chair,' said Charles.

'Oh, is it?'

'Green and white, dear.'

'This, Charles, is lamp-post and park-bench colour, but not green.'

'I admit I know nothing of furniture, but I was told this is a masterpiece of chair-making.'

'Yes, Charles dear, no doubt about that, but it is such a hideous sight it will take me weeks to remove it from my memory.'

'Well, if I wanted to, I could have it in any other colour—red, beige, or in dark blue corduroy.'

Elsie put her hands to her head. 'Charles, p-l-e-a-s-e—'

'What's wrong with that chair?'

'Charles, there are certain things we do not agree on, and one of them is furniture. Now I want that chair out of the house. Immediately.'

'But where should I put it, Elsie dear?'

'Haven't you somewhere, a little hideaway, where you can put it?'

'You know I haven't any hideaway.'

'Well, Charles, it isn't going to stay here, that is certain.'

'Well, may I have it in my room?'

'Oh, that room is already so awful as it is—with the smell of cigars—but all right, Charles, for the time being, put it in your room and try and find a place for it outside this house.'

Coombs appeared with the tray of cocktails.

Elsie pointed to the corridor that led to Charles's room. The corners of her lips were pulled down as she said, 'Sir Charles has decided that he wants this chair in his room.'

'Very well, milady.' Coombs passed the cocktails around, and then, with the help of the footman, he carted the heavy chair down the corridor.

While the servants were still out of the room Elsie said, 'A man who is responsible for bringing anything like that into the world will not set foot in this house... Now tonight, Stevie, Mother is the Queen of the Ball. We're going to a wonderful place—well, not exactly a wonderful place. The house is a nice house—but neither you nor I would want it—but it's a nice house for the people who own it and something could be done to make it nice.

'The man who owns it has what is very important—he has the *bonne volonté*. He has the wish to improve his house, and that is something. He came to Mother and said, "Dear Lady Mendl, I want your advice," and he stated his problem. And Mother told him to give the party outside, instead of inside the house, in a tent, and not to make it just a Halloween party, for that is mostly for children, but to have a little entertainment. He was delighted, and Mother said that since we had a tent we might as well make it a circus. Well, he almost turned somersaults, the little man. I am not too happy about the brash colours of pumpkins and dead leaves, so the decorations on the table are green apples with silver leaves, and white candles.'

She looked at the clock. 'Are you coming with us, Charles?'

'I was asked to take some people, dear. You know, the party is far out in the Valley and everyone is short on petrol coupons, so I offered to take two people.'

Charles left to pick them up. Mother took Blue Blue and placed him beside her, and the car drove over the mountain in the direction of the San Fernando Valley, towards the house of

Mr Ringelnatz. As we descended the other side the tent became visible like a lamp in the dark distance.

Most of the guests were there when we arrived. It was the usual sharp and articulate group. The tense faces of the executives of the various motion-picture corporations and their wives, the happy faces of the clientele of the Mocambo and Romanoff's and the proprietors thereof, and the famous faces of stars.

The two coloured butlers were there, in white jackets, with the whites of their eyes big as pebbles, smiling broadly. They were singing out greetings and melodiously repeating the order for drinks; they were part of the merriment, shaking their heads with laughter at jokes and sailing forth with trays. They had extended themselves beyond their natural agility to a looseness and a degree of friendship completely uninhibited. They were happily drunk already, but since that was their normal state every night, they did their work efficiently.

Outside the tent large barbecue fires were burning, and there were two pumpkins on one, and a man in back of us said, 'I watched my kid yesterday cutting a face out of a pumpkin— made me sad. It seemed an awful long time ago that I did the same thing.'

Mother was kissed by everyone and led into the tent and placed at the foremost table. Mr Halvah was there already. He got up, which made him smaller than when he had been seated, and he came and bent over Mother's hand in continental fashion, and then twisted his head back into proper position. He had almost no neck and was a tightly fitted Napoleonic type. He adjusted his cuffs and twisted his head again, which seemed a fixed habit.

'This,' he said to the Swedish young woman who had
stood up, 'is the famous decorator, Elsie de Wolfe, now Lady
Mendl.' He completed the introductions to the six people Elsie
did not know. He twisted his neck again and said, waving
his hand, 'Lady Mendl is responsible for the exquisite décor.
Congratulations, Lady Mendl, it's beautiful.' He sat down. The
lady that sat between myself and him, Miss Delia Nordholm,
was a very healthy outdoor girl, with the eternally beautiful
face that one finds on Scandinavians. She wore a conservative
Alice-blue gown. She had a mass of golden hair done in an
old-fashioned way: it was piled on her head. She had a lovely
neck and snow-white skin. She looked like a Charles Dana
Gibson girl, fresh and guileless. Her blue eyes were clear and
her look direct. She was a young actress of great promise, and
she had to turn her head to listen to Mr Halvah, who spoke
to her in a low voice in spite of the blare of the circus music.

Charles arrived with two of what Mother called his 'ravishing creatures' and was seated at the equally important table
across the ring. Blue Blue had a ribbon in his hair and sat next
to Mother on a special chair. Mr Halvah had moved close to
Miss Nordholm; he had one hand on the back of her chair and
spoke with great insistence to her. There were streamers and
paper hats, noisemakers and balloons, and in the centre of each
table the green apples, silver leaves, and white candles. The
waiters were dressed in the red jackets of circus attendants, and
hawkers went about with trays of peanuts and candy.

The dinner started with shrimp cocktail, in heavy small
goblets placed on green paper doilies, a slice of lemon stuck
into the rim of the glass and the cocktail sauce poured over the
shrimp. This was followed by a choice of barbecued spareribs

with hot sauce, steak from the open fire, or roast chicken. After this came melon balls or ice-cream in fancy forms served in paper cups, and the coffee. The happy butlers ran around putting bottles of champagne on every table.

Some clowns came and ran into the audience, and a heavyset, red-haired woman in a blue-black sequin dress with a python draped about her wandered around. It all was gay and alive.

When the drums rolled and the lights went low a young acrobat went up a rope, hand over hand. He established himself on the trapeze and swung slowly back and forth. A roll of the drums commanded attention, and a spotlight went looking for him. A large ball was thrown to him, and after he had placed that on his forehead a smaller ball was thrown to him. He started the large ball spinning in one direction, placed the other on top of it and spun it in the opposite direction, and then stood up on the trapeze and swung back and forth without holding on to the ropes. To tremendous applause he slid down, bowed, and left the ring.

Next was a xylophone act, and then came ponies, trained dogs, and an animal act with a trainer dressed as a Hindu. He had a black panther and worked it without a cage. Four attendants stood at strategic posts with hands on gun belts. At the end of the act the panther lay on his back. The trainer went over and pulled open a zipper and a girl came out. The deception was very successful. This act earned the biggest hand. The girl climbed back into the panther skin.

'She's very beautiful,' said the Swedish girl as the panther cartwheeled out of the ring.

'She's all right, but you are the most beautiful thing I have ever seen, really,' said Mr Halvah and kissed her hand.

'Are you having a good time?' Mr Ringelnatz asked Elsie.

'It's perfectly wonderful,' said Mother.

The woman with the python came to the table.

'Isn't he beautiful?' said Mother, because the python was Mother's shade of green with white markings.

The woman had a great burden to carry. The reptile was draped about her in two sets of heavy coils that framed her large bosom. She had hold of it near the head. Its tongue was going incessantly.

'Well, now we have everything,' said Mr Halvah to the Swedish girl. She looked at him with her frank eyes. 'I mean, the serpent and apples—we can play Paradise.'

Mother was watching the show. A troupe of Chinese tumblers were performing.

Mr Halvah took an apple from the centre of the table and held it towards the python. The reptile moved its head away. Mr Halvah looked at the Swedish girl and said, 'He don't like apples. Do you like apples? I mean, apples from Paradise?'

She evaded the answer and asked the snake charmer if the snake had a name.

'Yes, his name is Ali,' said the woman and pressed the python's head close to her cheek. 'Give Mama a kiss,' she said. The python's tongue flitted out and back and out again.

'So it's a boy,' said Mr Halvah. 'So how can you tell the difference?'

Mother turned to me, and with the bad queen face she said, 'Look across the room, Stevie. If only once in my life I could have as much fun as Charles has every day of his life!' The plum face was rosy with gaiety, and he hugged himself as he leaned back to laugh.

Mother applauded the last act.

'I didn't know that snakes had sex,' Mr Halvah persisted.

'Everything has sex,' said the snake charmer meaningfully, raising one shoulder and one eyebrow.

'How can you tell it's a boy?' asked Mr Halvah.

The snake charmer made a motion as if she were getting out of a heavy jacket. She shifted the weight of the python and reached behind her to find its tail, and she turned to Mr Halvah and showed him—on the white, scaly underside of the reptile, about three feet from the tip of the tail—a bony slit that was like the thin edge of a pocketknife when the blade is snapped shut. She called it 'the spur'.

The Swedish girl looked away to the ring where a large black grand piano was being set up on a platform. Mother watched this also, with a dark face, fearing a concert number would follow.

The python had moved, weaving to this side and that, to maintain balance. Its coils started to move over the stout woman's body. Suddenly it straightened its neck, and its head was on the girl's bosom. It coiled, drawing its body after it, went under her arm, came up at the side of her head, rounded the neck and drew its body after it. For a moment the girl was paralysed with fear; then she let out a piercing shriek. She leaned back and lost balance and went down.

Mr Halvah grabbed the python, and the woman grabbed Mr Halvah and screamed, 'For God's sake, leave him alone! Take your hands off him!'

As soon as the girl fell, Blue Blue was on the floor like a streak and attacking the python. It was the game of the mongoose and the cobra. Blue Blue went for its throat, and fearlessly bit at its jaw, in quick jabs, like a prizefighter. He danced in, bit and flew back—and he took the python off the girl. The huge snake slid out into the ring, and Blue Blue jumped and backed and jumped and backed again. The python tried to lash the little dog with its body or smack him to the ground, and once it hit him. The dog drew the reptile on until the attendants came with equipment to catch it.

Blue Blue got an ovation. Mother held the trembling dog in her arms and patted him. 'Look,' she said, 'dear old Bloops, and he hasn't got a tooth in his head and by human standards he's almost eighty.'

The girl had been led out of the tent, followed by Mr Halvah. The host took Elsie on a round of the room.

'Without that wonderful dog that girl would have been a goner,' said Mr Ringelnatz.

In the centre of the floor a pair of seriously dressed concert artists appeared, and they played 'Chagrin d'Amour' loud and well; but after that the act went wild.

The piano player was bopped on the head and played sitting on the floor. The violinist started diving under the piano, and played 'Humoresque' while standing on his head on top of it.

Mr Halvah reappeared. He was unhappy and twisted his head on his short neck. He adjusted the cuffs of his shirt. 'She went home,' he said, twisting his cheap face into an expression of disapproval. 'You meet a dame like this once in a lifetime, and that's what happens. You go into a restaurant with her and everybody turns around. What shoulders—what legs—and what everything else is there?'

Mr Halvah engaged in the Hollywood pastime of reporting

with author's pride his intimate dialogue. He fastened his cuffs and gave a reading of these lines.

'I said something new to her.' He cleared his throat and twisted his neck. 'I said, "I don't want to know where you live—I don't want to know your telephone number. I just want to know when I can see you again, and at what hour."

'So she said, "Friday, at eight o'clock."

'But then I said to her, "Darling, that's a hell of a way off. What have we today?—Monday—and I love you."

'"I know," she said. "Friday, at eight."

'"I'll call for you," I said.

'"I thought," she said, "you didn't want to know where I lived."

'"That's right, dear, I will wait for you on a street corner, close to your house, as if you were a poor girl. I'll meet you under a lamp, like in Paris, in the rain, so I've got to know where you live. I'll take you home.

'"Ah!" I said, "I have known a woman exactly like you fourteen years ago, in Paris—and to think that you would come back to me, much more beautiful, and much more lovely than you were then." I told her the story of that other love, and she had tears in her eyes one moment, and she laughed the next. But she said it was still Friday.

'I think I did all right for the first day, but I still have a hell of a long way to go.'

He got up, for Mother was returning to the table, and she said that we had to leave.

Mr Halvah bowed over her hand and said, 'Good night, Lady Mendl, I had a wonderful evening, thanks to you and Blue Blue.'

'Now there's a nice young man. He has an aura about him,' said Mother. 'So rare these days. I must tell Charles to ask him to the house.'

6

To the One I Love the Best

Elsie had sent her car to pick me up at the studio. Sir Charles had come along, and he drove back with me to the house. As we passed through the M-G-M gate I noticed that the guard looked at the chauffeur with surprise, and then I saw in the rearview mirror that tears were running down the chauffeur's cheeks.

I asked, 'What's the trouble with Achille?'

Charles said, 'Awfully sentimental, these Italians,' and then he took the speaking tube and asked, 'I say, Achille, what part of Italy do you come from?'

'I come from no part of Italy, Sir Charles,' said Achille, and added, 'My real name is Joe. I was born and raised in Connecticut.'

'Well, it's remarkable the way you've been able to keep up that Italian accent, Achille.' Charles hung up and turned to me. 'Elsie is very upset. Blue Blue died this morning, and the butler left. You can always get another miniature poodle, but Coombs was a good man.'

He took the speaking tube again. 'I say, Achille, where is he gone—what's-his-name, Coombs?'

'He didn't say, Sir Charles. He just pointed in an easterly direction up the hill when I asked him where he was going.'

'Well, that might mean Mary Pickford or the Rathbones, or Otto Preminger, or it could be Atwater Kent or Mr Munchin, but I should say none of them are the type that go around stealing servants. Or am I wrong, Joe?'

'I'm afraid you are wrong, Sir Charles, but nobody didn't steal him, he wanted to go for weeks. You see, he don't like to sweep. He don't mind a little valeting, but no dusting or sweeping. He likes to be where he can dress up and give orders. He wants a house with twenty servants, not just six. But don't worry, Sir Charles, he'll be back. He'll miss those good leftovers.'

Sir Charles turned to me and said, 'Elsie's always talking about going back to Versailles when all this is over. Now, I like it here. You have everything, and comfort besides. I'd much prefer staying here. This climate agrees with me. I think the scenery is awfully pretty, and the girls one can have to lunch and dinner! In all the world there are no more beautiful women—blondes, reds, brunettes—and one can get almost anything to eat here. I find the restaurants exceedingly good, and one eats well at private houses.'

We got to the house in time to change and then went to the living-room. The candles were being lit, the room was ready, and Mother came down the stairs as usual. She wore one of her Mainbocher uniforms, and, as always at the beginning of the cocktail hour, she staggered a bit with age until she found somebody's arm. But then, after a while, the motor started; she always straightened up, kicked herself free, steadied herself, and was on her own. She pulled at her skirt so that it sat right; she pulled at it on both sides, like a little girl about to sit down in a new party dress, and she started her circle. As she did every day, she walked to one of her pictures first and then to her various toys, to her jade menagerie, her rose-quartz menagerie, and her crystal menagerie, to small statuary of gold and silver, and, finally, to a glass cabinet that held a collection of seashells. She arranged the various objects and talked to them. Her lips moved silently when she thought herself unobserved. Now and then, as if starting an argument, she yelled an unexpected, defiant 'Ha!' and sometimes she said loudly, 'What?' in a high voice. She seemed to have conversations with people invisible to the rest of us, and with her beloved objects of great beauty.

Between her and Sir Charles mostly one-way conversations took place. When Charles talked, it was always of realities and the world as it exists, and Elsie did not hear a word of it. When Elsie spoke, it was of the beautiful world, of Versailles, exquisite houses and furniture, Louis XIV and XV, Pompadour, Sheraton, Duncan Phyfe and the Adam Brothers, of flower arrangements, seating arrangements, still lifes and artists.

When at times she seemed a little sad, it was concern for a piece of furniture suffering from lonesomeness in some cold warehouse. And of these things and the goings-on in Elsie's paradise, Charles did not hear a word. Only upon repetition of the subject and an insistence upon attention could either get the other's ear.

'I met a most extraordinary man today,' said Charles to Elsie, who was arranging the elephants in her jade menagerie. 'Gallant Frenchman, colonel in the last war—like us, too old to fight in this one—lives in Benedict Canyon—a bona fide resident of Hollywood. Built himself a house and a pool—has some land there, and a cow. Good fellow.'

'Ha!' said Elsie. 'A cow.' She had politeness in her inattention. She picked up a word now and then and repeated it, and then went her own way again.

'His own milk,' said Sir Charles, 'cream and butter. He has started a small farm, with boxes of cement, and there he raises his own snails, and, in the brook on his property, small freshwater lobsters—which are called crayfish here. Excellent cook besides. Name is Count Bobino. He's coming here for cocktails. Elsie, he's bringing a friend, a very important man, and a great gourmet. They live for each other. The count cooks and the other eats, and they talk about the great meals they have had the way other men brag about their amours. Munchin is the name of the other one—French also—but he owns twelve hotels, international industrialist, steamship lines, he builds whole cities—and his appetite is tremendous.'

Elsie was with her seashells. 'How remarkable,' she said, for Charles had paused, and 'How remarkable' fitted almost any pause.

'Elsie dear, Mr Munchin once ordered dinner for six people. Hors d'oeuvres, soup, fish, meat, salad, dessert, and coffee. He said to the waiter, "Bring the hors d'oeuvres"—and he ate all six of them. And the waiter said, "Should I bring more?"'

'More what?' said Elsie, arranging the shells.

'"More hors d'oeuvres," the waiter said. "No, bring the soup for everybody," said Munchin, and he ate all the soup, the fish, the six meats, the sweets, cheeses, salads—and the waiter asked, "What about the other people?" And Munchin said, "Oh, they'll be along later. Give me the bill for this and let them pay for their own dinner.'"

The footman announced Count Bobino, who had come without his friend. Mr Munchin, he explained, had got hungry again. There was a fabulous new *charcuterie*, a German delicatessen, near the Farmers Market, where every kind of sausage could be had, and this had been discovered by Mr Munchin. He had stopped and ordered a liverwurst sandwich, liverwurst being the speciality of the house. The proprietor had sliced a French type of bread, for Mr Munchin had shown him how large he wanted the sandwich, and then had put a large sausage into the meat-slicing machine with the circular, rotating knife. But he could not make the sandwich, for as the slices came off, Mr Munchin picked them up with his fingers and ate them. He ate almost the entire liverwurst, and the count could not get Munchin out of the delicatessen store. He wrote down the address and said that there was the best assortment of spices, of things in sour sauces, of hams, a mountain of the most delicious rosy smoked cuts of loins of pork, and every sausage imaginable.

The count then explained that he had made a great culinary discovery. 'I have found a hill where sour grass grows,' he announced poetically with a great sweep of his right arm. He turned to Elsie. 'The queen of all the soups in the world, as you know, dear lady, is Germiny à l'oseille. I have succeeded in raising almost everything I need for it. Also my farm produces the eggs and butter. You take the yolks of six eggs, which you dilute with a quarter pint of cream; put on the fire and stir until the preparation gives signs of boiling. The sour grass—which is really a kind of sour leafy plant called sorrel—you take three ounces and shred them and cook them in butter ahead of time, and add to the one and one-half pints of white consommé, and then the yolks of the six eggs with the cream, and stir all this until it reaches the boiling point. But do not let it boil.'

Elsie listened politely but heard nothing of what was said. Normally she was interested in cooking and especially in soups, but now she was thinking of other things, most probably her dog. The count paused.

She was polite again. 'But these things run into money,' she said. 'The cow and all that.'

'Ah, but dear lady,' said the count, arranging his monocle, 'the cow is always there. You have it for years.'

'Of course,' said Elsie.

The count got up. 'Dear lady,' he said, bending over Mother's hand, 'milk and cream and butter are rare now. You will allow me to send them to you. And as for the consommé, I have made a great discovery. As you know, Lady Mendl, the basis of consommé is the chicken. The old way, you had to buy two soup chickens. You had the trouble of cooking them. It takes hours, it's tiresome. You know what I do now? I buy canned noodle soup. I throw the noodles away—I don't want them—and begin with what is left. The can of noodle soup is only twenty or thirty cents.'

Elsie got up. She thought he was leaving and she staggered towards the door and she smiled, but the count was an intense man. He talked about his cow; the barnyard odour moved back into the house. Elsie was smiling bitterly, and there was no way of rescuing her; he had a firm grip on her arm. He walked her around the room.

Finally she took a stance and stopped him by saying firmly, 'You must take me to see your lovely farm someday.'

He kissed her hand once more and backed out of the room, promising to send eggs, snails, crayfish, butter, and sour grass. After he was gone Elsie said, 'What a charming, generous man, but the next time I wish he'd have cocktails with the cook. And how fortunate that what's-his-name, his friend, the Empty Stomach, didn't come along.'

Charles went to his room. Mother went to her little red clock and passed her white-gloved hand over it. 'Ha!' she said, and 'What?' and then the maid brought her coat and said that the car was waiting.

Elsie sat down on the couch, next to me, and, leaning on my shoulder, said in a dry voice, 'Stevie, something awful has happened to Mother. Bloops is gone.'

She got up and walked into her small salon, where she had always sat with Blue Blue while playing cards.

One evening, during cocktails, while she played gin rummy with Baron Henkell Donnersmark, I had sat on the sofa and I had fed half a cocktail sausage to Blue Blue. Elsie took her eyes from the cards at that moment. She wore no glasses, but she saw in the small mirror in that room, which was twenty feet away, and counting the reflection, another twenty, that I had given half a cocktail sausage to Blue Blue. She dealt a new hand and, looking at her cards with the bad queen face, she wagged her finger and said, 'All right, Bloops, if we're going to make a pig of ourselves at cocktails we'll go without dinner tonight.'

Now she sat alone. Charles came into the room and said that it was no use being sad about Blue Blue. 'Take a warm bath, dear, and go to bed for an hour, and you'll feel better.'

'I've ordered the car and Stevie is coming with me, and we'll drive around to some nice boys I know. They specialize in making stones for dogs, and we'll go there and order something that is fitting.'

We drove along into Coldwater Canyon and over the hills to the address of the stonecutters. Mother put her hand on my arm and said, 'Stevie, tell Mother what to put on Blue Blue's stone.'

I thought for a while and then I said, 'I'm never any good at things like that. I can't be spontaneous. I'll try, but I don't think I'll come up with anything that is any good.'

So we rolled in silence for a while, and then Mother said, 'How is this: "To the one I love the best"?'

I said that I'd be very happy if anybody ever put that on my stone.

The two young men who specialized in memorials for dogs showed various catalogues of appropriate stones and made sketches, and finally a simple plaque was chosen.

One of the young men suggested that the inscription read 'To the one I loved the best.'

'No,' said Elsie, 'Bloops has only checked in his little skin, I will always love him, and everybody at that party where he fought the python will remember him, and as long as you are remembered you are still around. Make it "To the one I love the best".'

Bloops had always sat up front. Tears were running down the chauffeur's face again.

'Italians are fortunate,' said Elsie. 'They can always cry it away or sing it away or love it away.'

We drove back to the house, and Elsie said she wanted to be alone. Charles was dining with a ravishing creature. Sadness made me hungry. I got in my car and drove to the delicatessen shop to buy myself a liverwurst and bread and a case of beer, and I took everything out to the shack on Topango Beach.

When I arrived there it was cold outside. I made a fire and sliced some bread. I looked out through the windows, which on beach houses are always coated with a smear left by fog and salt spray. In the violet hues of the California evening the lights of Venice and Santa Monica blinked far to the left, and along the coast the endless rosary of carlights started in motion. For a brief moment a school of fish passing in front of the shack silvered the dark water. Seagulls all facing in the same direction took off into the wind after the fish. Down over me sank the black mood of despair, to which the worry about things one should have done and did not do always adds itself.

A few of the seagulls came back. They landed near a piece of driftwood. I had no appetite and went out and put the sausage on the wood. The gulls hopped around it, fighting, screaming and tearing at it, and trying to carry it off; suddenly they stopped and left the sausage alone. Heidi, a Saint Bernard who lived at the end of the beach, was approaching slowly with the big carpet-slipper-like feet and the dumb, kind, deadpan face. She walked to the sausage, sniffed it slowly, inspected both ends of it, and then carefully picked it up in her teeth. With the seagulls following her overhead, she swayed up the beach and, among the pilings that supported an old house, she slowly ate it.

There was a decrepit, comfortable chair in the shack made of bundles of bamboo tied together and then bent so as to make two sides and an intricately woven back. Into this frame some kapok had been stuffed, covered with a faded chintz. This piece of furniture was representative of the entire place. There was a couch related to it in design, large, and also leaning in all directions. This was covered with sackcloth.

Up the beach, a hundred yards or so away, was a little hide-out of red brick, neat and simple, and there one could always find consolation. It belonged to Fanny Brice. There was a light in the window. Fanny Brice was a regular morning visitor, coming to the shack around ten, with a sketch or a half-finished painting. She had a son who had much talent and painted in town. She made bouquets of flowers and individual flowers that were sweet and sentimental.

She was holding her jaw when I got to the house and she yammered, 'Oh, my gad, I had a terrible experience with my teeth. I had jackets put on them, Loodvig. Oh, I looked beaudifool, nice teeth like an ad for toothpaste. And then I went to my next radio show and I tried to do the baby talk and—would you believe it?—I stood there in front of the mike and I almost died, I couldn't talk. So I went back to the dentist and I said, "You gotta do something to these teeth. File 'em down or something." So I stepped in the chair and he filed, and then I went and tried rehearsing. But it didn't work. Then I went back again, and he filed some more, and I tried again. I couldn't even say "Momma", so I said, "Maybe it's my ears that's wrong—I'll have it taken down. Let's make a recording." So I made a recording and I played it back. Well, it wasn't me at all. I went back, and the dentist said, "Fanny, I can't file them any more. I'm down to the stumps now and you'll have a terrible toothache. You'll be sensitive. The jackets are too thin." Well, you know what happens now? The whole front row has to come out and I have to wear a plate. Don't talk to me about caps!'

As I walked back in the sand towards the shack on the beach I saw the headlights of a big car feeling its way down the road towards Topango Beach. It stopped, then moved on, and the lights came in thin strips through the bamboo fence that enclosed the shack. When I got there Achille approached, walking over the dried leaves of the eucalyptus trees.

He handed me a letter and looked around, fascinated by the surroundings. 'So that's where you hang out,' he said, adding 'sir' after a pause he never made when talking to Sir Charles.

The note was in Elsie's bold hand, written, as was all her personal correspondence, in green ink on a card with a green border and a golden crest and an engraving of a small, elegant wolf's head. The note said: 'The world belongs to the living, Stevie. Take me out, but let's dine somewhere I've never been before, like Mocambo.'

So I went up to the petrol station and called up the Mocambo and said that Lady Mendl wanted to dine there this evening.

The head waiter said, 'Anything for Lady Mendl.'

'Have you Germiny à l'oseille, the sour-grass soup?'

'I have time to make it.'

I ordered the rest of the menu, then said, 'A little table for two, and a bottle of champagne.'

When we arrived at the Mocambo there was no doorman on the pavement, nobody to show us inside, nobody in the cloakroom. In the entrance hall of the place stood a couch made of artificial grass which a cleaning woman was brushing. In the large room itself all the chairs stood on the tables, and a chef was annoying the tropical birds in the large glass cages

overhead by throwing a napkin up at them, catching it as it
floated down, and then throwing it again. In the centre of the
dance floor stood a little table with a lighted candlestick on
it and two places set, and a bottle of champagne was on the
ice, in a stand at the side. The head waiter came, still in street
clothes. He said, 'I am awfully sorry.'

Elsie looked around the room and said, smiling, 'I have
never seen a better crowd in Hollywood.'

The head waiter then explained that they were a supper
club and that the help arrived late.

The food was very good, and so was the wine. I don't know
what Elsie did with what she drank; she must have had hollow
bones. That night we consumed three quarts of wine, and
I drank only half of it. Disciplined, she sat as straight as the
candle on the table. Only towards the end of the evening did
she become a little tired. After one of the many visitors to the
table had left she said, 'Who does that man work for again?'

I said, 'For M-G-M.'

It was Louis B. Mayer. And when the actor Herbert Marshall
had paid his respects to her and gone back to his own table,
limping very slightly because of his artificial leg, Mother said to
me, 'You know, Stevie, that poor dear man has a withered arm.'
And then she said, 'Oh, Stevie, Mother is so grateful you're on
this boat with her. Let's go to our cabins now, and—think of
it!—tomorrow at this time we'll be in Versailles.'

She fell asleep in the car, and when we got home Achille
carried her upstairs.

I couldn't sleep, and I found among the books on my desk
an album of the Villa Trianon in Versailles that Elsie had
made. It was filled with photographs of the house, the gardens

and the pool, and there was also a photograph of a little dog cemetery, and there was a plaque somewhat like the one we had ordered this afternoon. It was to the memory of another dog, and it read: 'To the one I love the best.'

Mother had again been extemporaneous.

7

You Shall Have Music

Through the corridor that led to Sir Charles's room came the strains of his rich voice, from a phonograph. It was a good voice; it was for a vast auditorium, like Carnegie Hall.

'Shut the door, please, Coombs,' Mother said to the butler. But the voice still came through the door. It had the volume and resonance of Melchior in his richest timbre. Sir Charles was rendering one of his favourite Lieder, called 'Ich grolle nicht, wenn auch mein Herz zerbricht'.

He usually sang it when he thought he was alone in the house. He sang it frequently. The first time I heard it was one evening when I came in early from the beach for dinner. After parking my car I decided to walk up and down outside the house. There, suddenly, I heard the moans of someone in acute distress. Entering the house, I saw Sir Charles, seated alone in the salon beside a phonograph. He was listening to a recording of his own voice; the machine had been running too slowly at first and had produced the sounds of moaning. When he saw me he nodded silently, the way one does in a concert hall after the music has started, and motioned me to a seat.

Now Charles was playing the record in his room. The machine ran properly and the melody was pure and strong and in the best Liedersinger tradition. It came full-throated through the corridor. Elsie was holding her head. Without being told, Coombs closed the large glass french doors that led out into the garden, but the voice maintained itself.

'Oh, the musical agonies I suffer!' said Elsie. 'Concerts bore me to death, and when one of the guests sings or plays the piano after dinner, it's torture. And here we are, in Hollywood, and in no other place in the world would you find in one city, at the same time, Horowitz, Rubinstein, Heifetz, Stravinsky, Stokowski, and that terrible Schönberg—and then people like Bing, who sing, and what's-her-name—Jeanette MacDonald—all very nice and all egomaniacs about their talent.

'Now, I love the silent arts, Stevie. When other people dream about love, or music, I dream about beautiful objects, about pictures and houses. Even when I was a young girl I did that.'

The butler opened the door and ushered in a man who delivered a gift-wrapped case. Elsie indicated where she wanted it and told the butler to open the case.

'There is one kind of music I tolerate, and that is decorative music. By that, Stevie, I mean a quartet, put somewhere out of the way, in front of a nice Watteau panel—in costume, white wigs and silver buckles—or else behind a screen. That, yes; it's nice to have them play while the guests arrive, and it kills the noises of the service during dinner.'

The butler had undone the wrapping, and Elsie pointed to the wooden case and asked, 'What's in it, Coombs?'

'Twelve quarts of cointreau, milady.'

'What will I do with twelve quarts of cointreau?'

The butler pondered the problem and then his face became animated. 'Give a party, milady,' he said with a French jerk of his head.

'Of course,' said Elsie. She turned and faced me, and took a determined step forward, and her right hand reached for my left shoulder to steady herself and grabbed a handful of cloth. She held up a handkerchief with her free hand and waved it like a flag. She made *chk-chk* and said, 'Stevie, Mother is going to do something for you. You know that enthusiasm in this world comes always fifty years too late to do the artist any good. Now, you don't care to be famous when you're dead and gone. You want what the world can offer you now.' She stamped her foot. 'And Mother is going to see that you get it. She will introduce you to the *beau monde*—you'll have a coming-out party. We'll get up a very careful list of people, and then we'll have a dinner for you, and by the time they serve coffee you can name your own price for your pictures, because you will be famous.'

The butler came with a silver tray and presented a letter that had arrived with the liqueur. Mother glanced at it. 'Now, isn't that thoughtful of dear Monsieur Cointreau. Here, read.'

The note was in French, from M. Cointreau's New York agent, and said:

Dear Lady Mendl,

Among the many things you have done in your long and shining career is one for which I am particularly grateful, and that is that you have made our liqueur, as an ingredient of the Lady Mendl Cocktail (1/3 gin, 1/3 grapefruit juice, 1 jigger of cointreau), world famous. *Alors*, I am most happy to send you this case of cointreau—with the assurance of etc... etc...

Elsie's face toughened and the voice went dry. She waved the letter as she handed it back to the butler, saying, 'Charming letter, but if this is followed by a request for an endorsement and a picture of me without having to pay for it, we will say politely, "*Non, merci beaucoup*".'

She grabbed my shoulder again. 'Listen, Stevie, to what Mother says: Never let them run over you! Now we shall get busy with the menu, and after that with the list, and then send out the invitations. All we have to buy is a little champagne. The food Mother is going to pay for. Now, how do you like this for the menu? We'll keep it very simple.

'We'll start with soup—and Susan makes something very delicious, an oyster soup, and she has some kind of speciality that is served with it. The fish we dispense with, as oysters are both fish and soup and we want to keep it simple. The next thing is duck, which we can get without ration points, and with this we serve the small French peas with onions.

'For dessert we'll have chocolate soufflé. I myself never eat any dessert, but most people like it, and for ices it's too cold in California at dinner time. A few flowers aren't going to cost too much.'

Sir Charles's record had finished playing. Mother was a woman for direct action. She immediately sent the butler to inform Sir Charles that there would be a party. Sir Charles arranged the seating of the guests and worried about all problems of protocol whenever a party was given. The secretary was informed, and the cook. Elsie was smiling, for, as Charles had said, she loved nothing so much as a party.

A few days passed, and Mother added people to the list, and it was getting bigger and bigger. The weather was fine, and she decided that it could be held half inside, half outside, the house. She said, 'We'll place the rugged ones like Gary Cooper and Clark Gable outside,' and then she added softly, 'I think we ought to have a little music, Stevie.'

I said, first of all, that Mother hated music; secondly, that all the brilliant and artistic people in town were on that list, who would make conversation; and, most important, that there was a war still going on and it wasn't the time for too much gaiety.

Mother looked at me a little hard at first, but then she kicked me in the ribs with her elbow and said, 'You're right, Stevie. The brilliant people can make brilliant conversation, and this is no time for dancing and high jinks—why have music? Oh, you're so right, Stevie. What would Mother do without you to advise her? It's your party, dear, and everything must be exactly as you want it.'

Charles had been listening, and when we were alone he said to me, 'You know, dear boy, you're going to have music at your party. You know that, don't you? And what's more, you'll pay for it. One cannot win a war with the old girl. Watch out now, and remember what I said.'

It was a week before the party, and I was up in my room. Some people had arrived for cocktails, and suddenly I heard music below. On the way to the living-room I met Charles. I said, 'I was shaving upstairs just now, and it seemed to me that I heard some music. Did you hear any?'

'Yes, of course. That's your music, dear boy, no doubt. Elsie is having a rehearsal of some kind. I told you you cannot win a war with the old girl.'

The butler passed, and Charles said, 'Who's making music, Coombs?'

'Milady is trying out an orchestra, Sir Charles,' he said. 'For the party.'

'What did I tell you?' Charles walked to the bar, and when he came back he said, 'She's an incredible woman. She has solved the problem so that we're having music and doing something for the boys at the same time. Come and see.'

In a corner of the bar sat three sailors. One, a thin, long boy, was bent over a big guitar, which he called a 'ghi-tar.' The second had a small concertina and hummed through his nose. And the third played on a clarinet. They played cowboy songs, sad and muted.

The guitarist got up and said they would bring a little of that Texas sunshine into the house, and they sang 'Pistol Packin' Mama' and then little-dogie songs, and while strumming the guitar the tallest did some Western yodelling.

'Now you can't possibly object to that,' said Elsie. 'And I hope it settles all your worries about the war, and all these dear boys ask for is a little drink and a ten-dollar bill each, that makes it thirty dollars—now that's not too much for an evening's entertainment.' Elsie looked like the bad queen again, and left us.

Charles sat down and said to me, 'Usually I'm the victim. This time she's done it to you. I offer ten quid if you can get out of paying for the music.'

We were, that evening, only the family at dinner, and Elsie said, 'Now, Stevie dear, you haven't told Mother how you liked the orchestra.'

I hesitated.

'It's a gay note,' said Elsie and continued, 'Remember, Charles, those Neapolitan street singers we had in Venice, in their lovely costumes? Why, people went perfectly mad over them. They're fond of things like that. I'd say let's have them, now that I have found these boys who will come in their Navy suits. Well, Stevie?'

I said, 'Look, Mother, I give up. I don't want any music, but you do—'

Mother looked a little hurt. She said, 'Why don't we do this? We'll each pay for a musician. Stevie, you pay for one, Charles pays for one, and Mother pays for one. Now, that's very fair, don't you think?'

'I don't mind at all,' said Charles and walked out of the room.

'I say,' he said to me later in the corridor, 'that's awfully cheeky of the old girl! And why do you let her do it? Why don't you put your foot down?'

'I'm sorry,' I said. 'It's not a complete defeat, but I lost the battle and I owe you—how much is ten quid?'

'Under these circumstances I wouldn't dream of holding you to it. She can make unholy complications. Anyway, we have a fine evening to look forward to—this dinner. Oh Lord, I've done the tables—you have all the crashing bores at yours with Elsie. I've had to sacrifice you to them. I've saved myself. I have Mary Pickford on my right and Olivia de Havilland on my left, Nadia Gardiner *en face*, Anita Colby and a new one'—he pulled out his notebook and put on the pince-nez and looked for the name—'Arlene Dahl. That makes a nice table.'

The night before the party Mother's maid came to tell me that Lady Mendl wanted to speak to me.

Mother had a bed which was an antique, and beautiful. She also had a great liking for lying on the floor, on a mattress covered with fur blankets. There she rested, supported by many pillows. On this mattress she exercised in yogi fashion, and occasionally stood on her head.

The room was softly lit. A fire burned in the chimney, and the one maid who refused to call Mother 'milady' was arranging the pillows. Elsie punished her by calling her 'Miss Bridget'. The 'Miss' was like a hiss.

Mother was a wonderful portrait, like a very complicated rich little Christmas tree, beautifully ornamented, delicate, glittering here and there with jewels; she still had the white gloves on her hands, and a turban about her head. She gave instructions to *Miss* Bridget to bring two rum punches. Then she said, 'Are you satisfied, my dear, with the list of the guests? I don't think we have any deadwood. Only Charles has invited some awful people, that woman from Hungary—Hanky Panky or what's-her-name—and he wanted the monster, the Empty Stomach, who is fortunately unable to come—oh dear, Stevie. Anyway, we have a nice table. I've chosen the people myself.'

Miss Bridget brought the drinks. Mother smiled. 'Put the light on the Virgin, *Miss* Bridget.'

The upper part of the room was in darkness. Miniature spotlights lit up small mirrors, flowers in vases, and now a sweet, very modern Madonna set in a mirrored frame.

'No, a little more to the right—good, now leave it that way, *Miss* Bridget. Thank you so much.

'Night is important, Stevie, because then you can light up things. Now, there is a wonderful man that Mother knows. Mother calls him "Nighty"—his real name is Mr Nightingale, and so fitting—he functions at night. Because he belongs to the night he's the most perfect musician—what am I talking

about? I have musicians on the brain—I mean, electrician. Mr
Nightingale is the most perfect electrician for the night, when
you need them most—and, for that matter, also for the day. If
ever you want to have anything done, call him.

'Now, dear Stevie, I have engaged Mr Nightingale to light
up the house and the garden tomorrow night. It will be a little
like Versailles.' She smiled sadly. 'Dear Stevie, give Mother
your hand. Would you terribly mind if Mother asked you for
a great favour?'

'No, not at all.'

'Stevie dear, do you mind if Mother gets a few people to
make a little quiet night music?'

I said that I didn't mind and that we had all agreed on the
sailors. Mother fell asleep, smiling.

Next day Mr Nightingale was busy wiring trees, the house
was torn apart, and all was upset. I went to Charles's room.
He looked up as I entered and then tripped over boot trees
and shoes. He scattered them with a kick of his foot. John had
been sent to get extra chairs, and Charles was helpless. He was
wearing grey felt bedroom slippers and magnificent British
underwear, wool, and white, and reaching from the ankles to
his middle, and an upper piece with sleeves to his wrists. The
number 38 was embroidered in red on it.

'What does the number on your underwear mean?'

'That's the year one bought it, dear boy, so one can keep
track how long it lasts. I had this made in thirty-eight, and
now we are forty-five—that's not bad. Of course, it's made in
England, Hilditch and Key, Piccadilly.' He pointed to a small
tab and attached clasp beneath the knee. 'This is to hold up the
socks. It's attached to the underwear, so you don't have to wear

those awkward garters. And this tab here below the stomach is another good thing. It keeps your shirt from riding up on you. And this band in the middle here—you lace it a bit, and it keeps you in shape. Now that's proper underwear for you.

'About tonight, you'll be lucky, dear boy, if you don't end up with Carmen Cavallero and his orchestra playing for dinner. Let me warn you, be prepared for surprises.'

A few borrowed butlers and some men who worked for a caterer named Shields arrived, and it slowly got dark. Parties mean worry and are a great responsibility, especially when half of the guests are to be under the open, unpredictable California sky.

The hairdresser and his assistant arrived, and Elsie went upstairs to get dressed. Charles met me on the way to my room. He had a box of cigars and a bottle of whisky in his hands. He said, 'I want to tell you that I am very fond of you,' and he added, somewhat embarrassed, 'I must ask you a favour, something personal. Would you mind coming to my room for a second where we can talk?'

In his room we sat down.

'The other day when we were at your little place on the beach with that ravishing creature, you made sport of me. I appreciate that you did it in front of me, but you told a story of how one day, coming early for dinner, you heard moaning inside the house and then found me listening to a recording of my own voice. I know you don't mean to hurt me, but women have no sense of humour—they believe stories like that.

'Now, dear boy, please don't tell that story again—you see, you must understand. It's the only thing I do really well, I assure you. Now I might be moved to sing a song or two tonight after dinner—you don't mind, do you? But you see, if while singing I looked at the audience and saw you leaning over to whoever is next to you, I'd know immediately that you were telling that fib again and my throat might go back on me. You know, I studied for years, with de Reszke, who said that I had an excellent voice. He even went so far as to say, "Why don't you make a career of it, Charles?"'

He got up. We were both relieved that it was over. He handed me the box of cigars and the bottle of scotch. 'This is for your party, dear boy.'

I went to dress, and when I came down the trees were lit up: the effect was as if green leopard skins were hung over the branches. The candles flickered, and the first guests arrived. They were a young and handsome couple in love, and to be married in a few days. She was pretty and a starlet, and the man was a very decent-looking and much decorated captain in the Air Force. They went to the bar and drank their cocktails.

Then down the stairs came Elsie, and she was magnificent—more royal than all the queens reigning at that time. She had over her shoulders a long pale blue cape such as the officers of the French Foreign Legion wear. She was dressed in snow-white, and wore all her medals, including the Croix de Guerre for her service in the field in the First World War. She wore a pair of long gloves, white, with jewels embroidered on them. The right glove had a diamond surrounded by blue stones; the left, a sapphire bracelet, in her hair she wore golden leaves, and she had on her big Indian necklace.

Two policemen came in and said that they were going to take care of traffic outside, and they each got a drink, and then there was commotion in the kitchen, and Mother said, 'The only person that has a right to be temperamental in a house is the cook. Poor Susan has been working all day yesterday and today, and she prepared something special to go with the soup, and it's very delicate, and one of the men must have knocked it off the oven. And now she will be in a dreadful state. Go out and pacify her. Say a few nice things to her, Stevie.'

When I got back the announcer had taken his place and the party was at its beginning. Suddenly Mother said, 'Stevie, what about the music?'

The announcer pronounced, 'Mr Gilbert Miller, Mr and Mrs Rubinstein... Mr Pinza... Miss Leonora Corbett, Mr Charles Boyer... Mrs Whitney...'

'Good evening... *bon soir*... *bon soir*...' Mother made brief conversation with the guests and introduced me. There was a pause, and then we heard music, a faint strumming barely audible over the hum of conversation. Mother said, 'Go, Stevie, and tell them to play a little louder.'

I went to where the music came from and saw that there was only one sailor, the one with the guitar, and I asked him where the others were. He said that they couldn't come because they had got drunk and were in the brig.

I went back to Mother.

'Miss Jeanette MacDonald... Sir Alexander Korda...' 'Good evening... good evening...'

In the next pause I told Mother about the missing sailors. I was sorry, I said, but only one musician had shown up. Charles came over. Elsie was, at the moment, introducing me to a newly arrived goddess. Charles waited, and then said, 'Elsie, did you know that only one of the musicians has come? The others appear to be in lockup.'

'I know, Charles dear,' said Elsie, and to Marlene Dietrich she said, 'I don't know what I'd do without dear Charles—he worries about every detail when we give a party.' She looked at him and smiled her smile of dismissal, but Charles stayed, he wanted to ask something.

'Yes, Charles dear?'

'I say, whose musician is it, the one that's come?'

Mother pulled up her gloves. 'Oh,' she said with the bad queen face, 'not my musician, Charles, and certainly not Stevie's musician. It's your musician that came.'

8

A Thing of Beauty Is a Joy Forever

The day after the party Mother came and spoke to me in a new tone, the way my own mother had talked to me when I was very small. She did not exactly say, 'Wash your hands and behind the ears, and put on a clean shirt.' She said, 'Now, Stevie, Mother has some very important people coming to lunch. These people were here yesterday at the party, and Mother talked to them. They are going to buy one of your pictures, and they are very rich.'

Charles came into the room.

'Mr and Mrs Fruehauf are coming to lunch,' said Elsie. 'They're very nice.'

'Of course they're nice,' said Charles. 'They're Texans. All Texans are nice. They're very well off.'

Mother turned to me. 'Now, Mother wants you to bring some pictures, the ones you like best.'

I said that I had only one picture that was finished.

'What's the subject, Stevie?'

'It's a picture of a flower, and a piece of bamboo screen, and a little ocean in back of that.'

'That sounds perfect,' said Elsie. 'Is it a watercolour?'

'No, it's an oil.'

'That's exactly what they will want. It's not too large, I hope?'

'No, it's about—' I showed the size with my hands.

'Oh, a fireplace picture! That's what they will like.'

It was a picture I was happy about. I had stopped at a sidewalk flowerstand on the way to the beach, and there in an old rusty can was a flower of intense yellow with a velvety pale-green leaf. I had bought it for twenty-five cents and taken it to the beach. I had placed it on the window sill on the porch; in back of it was an old split bamboo window shade. The background was a strip of beach and some fishing boats with people.

'Well, Stevie, you get this picture and have it here by lunchtime, and then we will make our first sale. Now, Mother wants to do that for you, and she doesn't want a cent of this money— no commission. It's all for you.'

I drove down to the beach and got the picture. I took it into the house. Charles asked to see it, and I took it to his room. Something awful gets into the face of an Englishman of Charles's type when he looks at a painting. He looked at it as people do at a bum who is asking for a handout.

'I daresay I know nothing about painting,' he began, 'so don't take my judgement. Now, the flower I like. That's very good, and the leaves, but that rusty tin can—'

'That's the way it is.'

'Well, couldn't you have put it in a vase or a proper pot?'

'Yes, but I liked the colour of the can.'

He had an unhappy expression on his face. 'It isn't pretty, that's what I mean to say, and one has to think about what it is.' He looked at it with doubt. Then he said, 'Don't mind me—you know what Elsie thinks of my taste. Show it her.'

(He always omitted the 'to', saying, 'Give it me', 'Show it her'.)
'And it wants a frame, don't you think? At least, that is what
I think Elsie will say.'

We took it in to show to Elsie. Mother looked at it very
briefly. 'That's lovely,' she said, 'just lovely, Stevie,' and she
went on supervising the flower arrangement on the table.

Charles looked at the picture again. 'I say, Elsie, don't you
think it wants a frame of some sort?'

'Don't be difficult, Charles. Stevie's pictures don't need
frames. What's that brown dung?'

'That's an old can.'

'A can?'

'The flower is growing out of a rusty can.'

'Oh!' said Elsie. 'Have you given it a name?'

I said I hadn't.

'Well, that's not important,' said Elsie.

'You can't call it "Flower with Can",' said Charles.

'Well, just call it "Flower",' said Elsie. 'The shade of green
is lovely. The yellow has a little chartreuse light in it. I think
it's perfectly lovely.'

The butler announced the arrival of the Fruehaufs' car, and
I put the painting behind the sofa.

'Why do you hide it?' asked Charles. 'Put it where they can
see it. I say, you're not timid, are you?'

'Well, to tell you the truth, I am timid. I hate to face a room
full of people, and even more so people in small groups that
I don't know—especially under circumstances such as these.'

'I shall cure you of that instantly, dear boy. I was very timid
myself, and my late chief, Lord Tyrell, cured me of it. This is
the way it's done. Before entering a room, you take two deep

draughts of air and you say to yourself, "I am the equal of anyone in this room, and the superior of most." And then you march in. Try it out on these people. Go out there. Wait until you hear their voices and then come in. You'll find it works.'

I went out, then came back in, the superior of everyone in the room, and was introduced to a very pleasant couple—very nice, very kind, very jovial.

The lunch was served. There was much hearty laughter, for both Mr and Mrs Fruehauf loved life and were part of it, and I dreaded the passage of time that would lead to the moment when the picture would ruin this nice lunch.

Mr Fruehauf was an honest man, who seemed to have vast enterprises and spoke of his workmen with a fatherly interest. He had a frank eye, and he ate well and slept well. He said he got a little depressed just before lunch sometimes, or dinner, but that the moment his stomach was full he felt fine. Mrs Fruehauf laughed audibly at everything mildly funny, and I wished that behind the sofa I had a canvas of a Dutch landscape, with cows and a windmill, or a peasant girl with a crock going to the fountain, or a landscape in Tyrol—something that would not frighten them, for they were genuinely nice people.

The dreadful moment arrived. Mother led the conversation to the business at hand. Mr Fruehauf smiled happily in anticipation, and so did his wife, for both seemed to like me. The mood was good.

'Coombs,' said Mother, 'bring that picture.'

Coombs walked to the sofa and reached behind it. The picture wasn't even square. I had torn the paper from a larger sheet of drawing board, the upper edge was ripped instead of cut, and on the edges I had tried the colours, so that it was very untidy.

As she had done with the footstool of Madame Pompadour, Elsie asked Coombs to place the picture in the proper light. He leaned it against the back of the chair; it curved a little. Mr Fruehauf looked at it and said, 'Aha.' Mrs Fruehauf said that it was a lovely flower.

'You can do a whole room around that,' said Elsie, 'golden drapes, green paper. It's a very important picture.' And she asked a price for which they could have bought a horse. Elsie talked about the joy of owning a painting. She said that a thing of beauty is a joy forever, besides increasing in value every year.

Mr Fruehauf got up; his face was as blank as that of Charles when he had first looked at it. It remained blank as long as he looked at the whole. He studied the flower, then his eyes went down to the rusty can and there appeared two lines from the root of his nose running upwards and six others crossing it. He looked at his wife. 'Well, dear, what do you say? You wanted a picture.'

She nodded and said that she liked it.

'Sold,' said Mr Fruehauf simply, and sat down.

Strawberries had been served, and with them a bowl of powdered sugar. The bowl of sugar stood in front of me, and unconsciously I began to play with it, making a hill on one side and tracing a furrowed field on the bottom of the hill. The conversation wasn't free any more, and I could think of nothing to say. I continued, without knowing it, to play in my sugar garden. With some wafers that had come with the ice-cream I made a shack, and I took toothpicks and attached the small green leaves that are at the base of the strawberries and made some palm trees out of them. Nobody noticed it because I was protected by the centrepiece of flowers. Only Mother gave me a kick in the ribs, for Mr Fruehauf asked the second time, 'How do you want me to make out the cheque?'

I said, 'I am very sorry but I've changed my mind. The picture isn't for sale.'

Mr Fruehauf said something about the price, if I thought it was too low.

I said, 'No, no, on the contrary,' I merely had discovered that I was very fond of the picture and wanted to keep it for myself.

Everyone except Elsie and I was relieved.

'Maybe some other time,' said the kind Mr Fruehauf.

The party broke up. Mother went to her room without further comment.

But two days later I had to listen to a lecture. I was seated at the same table as Mr Halvah. With the coffee, Mr Halvah said that he had wanted to talk to me for a long time. He screwed his face into a mask of intense friendship and with concern deep in his eyes he motioned towards a flowered swinging couch on the patio at the far side of the pool.

'Oh, Bemmy,' he began, 'now you've got a good friend here, somebody who loves you like you was her own son—I don't have to tell you who that is, she's sitting over there, across the pool, she's looking at you now.' Mr Halvah waved his hand in the direction of Mother.

'We talked about you the other day, and they were all people who love you, important people, and you know, everybody got mad when we got around to how unpractical you are. Well, there are all these guys pulling down two hundred thousand a year and up, and you could do it playing, and what the hell, you just don't care. You lead a beachcomber existence; you're worse than Jello, you don't set, you won't stay still on one thing long enough. I mean it, you're always doing something new. When somebody wants to get a hold of you and pin you down, you're gone. Now I manage Bert—look at Bert! He does articles right and left for the big magazines. And you just get yourself into the slicks! If you worked a little more you'd get fifty thousand a serial, and the Book-of-the-Month, and a picture on top. It's those goddam jokes you put into your books—you're laughing yourself out of everything. You've got to be serious. Look at Hemingway! Look at Steinbeck! They don't tell jokes, they're very serious. You are killing yourself with jokes.

'Take Mr and Mrs Wallace of the *Reader's Digest*. They're serious people. Now, Bert said to me, "You know, there would be a job for Bemmy, in Paris. He's the ideal man. He speaks French, he has entrée into every circle, he speaks German and Italian, he knows Europe inside out and has friends everywhere."

'That job in Paris would mean a hundred thousand a year outright, and a suite at the Georges Cinq, and a chauffeur; all the entertaining, planes, servants, everything you ever dreamed of, and all the time to do things on the side. But you'd laugh yourself out of it again. If I took you up to meet Mr and Mrs Wallace you'd have them scared to death in a few minutes with your jokes. Now listen to me! Why don't you just laugh inside? Just think it, and don't say it, and don't write it—that's good advice. Look at Fulton Oursler! You know what that syndicated column will pay him? A hundred grand a year; and *The Greatest Story Ever Told*—at least another couple of hundred thousand. And you, in Hollywood—Bemmy, I could cry—why, you could have everything out here. Look at Bert! He has a house in New York, a home in Cuba, a home in Paris, a place in the country—and now he's in Japan being entertained by General MacArthur.

'Imagine yourself in his place. You're as brilliant as Bert, and besides that you can draw like a sonofabitch. And you'd muff it all in half an hour telling jokes to MacArthur. And that agent you have, for Christ's sake—how can anybody have an agent like that? You're pooling your business knowledge with his, which adds up to zero.

'And now this business about being a big brush artist—well, you can do that like Churchill when you're past seventy. I mean it—get yourself out of that papier-mâché existence.

'Look over there—see that bald-headed man? That guy is a very important man in the newspaper field. His wife used to be a beautiful model and a healthy girl. Now she's got to go to a hospital; she has a disease that's so complicated the Rockefeller Institute is backing her. But what I wanted to tell you is, when I talked to him about you he said, "He's a natural any time." Now a column is so easy—it's no work at all—you just knock it off while you're taking your bath.

'Now I have that girl, and she sits in a room when people talk, and she takes everything down, like an interview. She's a wonderful polyglot kind of girl—switches from one language to the other just like that. A hundred and fifty words a minute, and no mistakes. You should read her reports—she puts in everything, like "doorbell rings", "Mr Halvah answers the telephone"; and then the conversation and even things like "Maid enters with tray of sandwiches and iced tea", or "Mr Halvah gets up to wash his hands, will be just a minute". And all that time you don't even know she's there. You can imagine what you can accomplish. Well, you can have her any time.'

He straightened up from his confidential position, and I said very earnestly, 'What happens when two people have a conversation while Bert is talking on the phone? Or what happens to the priceless things you may say to yourself while washing your hands?

'There you are—see what I mean?—you're hopeless, because you don't believe in anything.

'Just one more thing, and I'll go. About your paintings. Here is that dear little old lady knocking herself out, giving you a party, trying everything to sell a picture for you. And, you build a garden in a sugar bowl and say that the picture isn't for sale. Listen! Most clowns would give their eye teeth to play Hamlet—and you do it the other way round—' He adjusted his clothes. 'I guess I'm just wasting my time. Well, go on laughing, Mr B., go on having a good time, but remember what I told you.' He gave me a sad look and then crossed to the side of the pool where in another flowered swinging couch Mother waited. He shrugged his shoulders so intensely that his coat collar rose over his ears, and then he disappeared into the house towards the bar.

I went over to sit with Mother.

'Did anything Mr Halvah said make any sense to you, Stevie?'

'No, Mother, he doesn't understand that humour is the most serious form of writing. Few people do—'

'I mean about the picture. I tried very hard to sell that, and Mrs Fruehauf wants it very badly now. They caked up and said if it was a matter of price they'd gladly pay whatever you asked.'

'Thank you, Mother, but I don't want to sell it. I'm not trying to be difficult—I'm deeply grateful to you—and now I'll tell you how I feel about painting.'

She put her chin in the palm of her hand and listened.

'I write to allow myself the luxury of painting. I am a painter and not a writer, and you will always see my books rather than hear them. I paint with type, and that is hard, for type has no colour, no variety beyond the dictionary and the stored information in the reader's mind. Like music, painting starts where words end.

'I have never attended one of my own exhibitions with any degree of pleasure. I always feel as if I were undressed and on exhibition myself. I always run away. I wish a way of acquiring pictures or dogs could be found other than by going into a gallery or a pet shop or buying them over a table.

'The Fruehaufs were nice people, but when I said the other day that the picture was not for sale, I said so because I felt sorry for them and for the picture. They would bore each other. A painter's pictures are like his children and his animals, he wants them to be loved. I have found, however, a way to satisfy myself. I have found a clear-eyed, critical, and hungry audience of people, all of whom are impressionists themselves, who love my pictures, who sometimes even eat them. They are children. I have discovered a method of writing a story, in the fewest possible words, and hanging pictures on to the text—pictures of flowers, of the night, of cities. They don't stop a minute to worry about rusty cans. I am doing one now with the cemetery of Père-Lachaise, with the tomb of Oscar Wilde, the Left Bank café Les Deux Magots, flowers, and the Seine. It's wholly satisfying to me, it makes me happy. I have found an art dealer who is an honest man, and I don't have to go to my exhibitions ever, or meet a client, and most of my pictures I give away anyway. Are you satisfied now, Mother?'

'Yes, Stevie, just one thing, just a mild suggestion. Mother was a very poor girl. Listen to Mother—money is important, not as such, but because of what you can do with it. And don't forget, Stevie, I never owed a red cent to an artist. I understand them, I love them, and I look after them. They are my true friends.'

9

The Iron Will

We were driving along Santa Monica Boulevard. 'You know, dear boy, sometimes life with the old girl is trying. She has a fixation that I snore. She says she can hear me breathe and talk in my sleep, she can hear me move around. Now, no one has ever complained about me. Her bedroom is just above mine, and she makes the fantastic claim that I keep her awake. She's talked to that housefly La Flèche about it, and he suggested to her that she let him soundproof my bedroom. That's cheek, you know. This morning they came and measured the ceiling, and they're going to put some cement or plaster up there that will deaden the noise.'

The chauffeur had turned his head and winked at a pretty girl.

Sir Charles took the speaking tube. 'I say, Achille, who was that you were smiling at?'

'I didn't smile at nobody, Sir Charles.'

'But I saw you. You smiled and you winked.'

'I mean, Sir Charles, I wouldn't smile at nobody for myself, sir. I mean, I wouldn't smile at any girl in the street just like that.'

'Well, who was that you smiled at then?'

'A young lady, Sir Charles, who smiled at the new car. I washed it this morning. And she smiled at you, sir.'

'She smiled at me, Achille?'

'Yes, Sir Charles. I wouldn't think of smiling back at nobody unless she smiled at you, sir.'

'Ha, ha! He's a card, Achille, a good man.'

Charles looked back out of the rear window of the car. 'Ah, it's Delia—ravishing creature—a child. Swedish. And the Swedish woman is all devotion and submission when she falls in love. She has talent, I am told, and so far she's fought off everybody here. She spoke to me the other day and she said that she was an orphan, and if ever she got married, would I give her away. I gave her a pat on the cheek and said I would, gladly.

'To get back to the business of noise,' Charles resumed. 'After all, Elsie is an American, and she has a sharp voice. I can hear the old girl when she's anywhere in the house. I can hear her pacing the floor. Naturally, it would never occur to me to complain or to have her room sound-conditioned. You know these American women's voices. They come from talking too loud. That's why everybody here has a sore throat. Now, you've never heard of a sore throat in the South of France or in Italy; it doesn't exist. They talk your head off, but in a low, melodious voice. The loud noises are part of marriage here; couples thrive on conflict. As for me, I love peace and quiet, especially in marriage, and, by God, in England you have it!

'One should always marry with the head, never with the heart. What I wanted to say is, that if instead of this life, which is all attention to the old girl, carting her from one place to the other, and standing by until all hours of the night because she never likes to go home, I would have occupied myself with serious business.

'You know, I had the ear of everybody. I am of some importance in England, I have good judgement, I have my income, and without my advice the old girl would have suffered grievous losses. If I had stayed on, it might have been better. I would have done very well, I would have got somewhere very high—and, mind you, I'm fond of the old girl, I don't say I'd be without her for a minute—but I wish I could get myself to say, "Now, look here, Elsie, stop that nonsense about putting this ugly ceiling in my room."'

He spoke through the tube again. 'I say, Achille, let's take the pretty way home.'

The pretty way was Sunset Boulevard.

'This will give me more time. You know, dear boy, I must put my foot down, really. I will put her against the wall, and I shall say something like this to her: "Now, look here, Elsie, this is the most ridiculous nonsense. No one in the world has ever accused me of snoring—we were taught to sleep with our mouths closed. Now, I'm not going to have this ceiling. I like my room as it is."

'I say, dear boy, they tell me that you can tear a house down with words. Could you think of something I might say to the old girl that would really take effect?'

He paused, and then said, 'No one has ever heard me snore. You know what happened? It's dashed impudent. I was in my underclothes the other morning when someone knocks at my door, a man comes into my room—has the gall to come into my room with measuring things and an assistant who holds the other end, just as if I weren't there. Those are the things that make life unbearable. Then Elsie comes down. I'm in my bathrobe by now, but in front of me she says, "What can we do to make this room more quiet?" That's all she said, but I won't forget it. I went into the bathroom.'

Charles's ripe-plum face went dark. 'I am going to have a good talk with the old girl as soon as we get home.'

We arrived at the house. In the living-room the carpet had been rolled back. Workmen carrying flat white fibre tiles with holes in them and bags of white plaster were passing through into Charles's room.

The room was in disorder—books and records and clothes stacked on a bureau, and the many shoes thrown into a corner. The bathtub was being used to mix the plaster in. The workmen proceeded to spread painters' cloths over the furniture.

'What a messy way to do things,' said Charles.

There were two plasterers in white overalls, large men, with the faces one sees on locomotive engineers. They smiled, and one of them said, 'Yeah, we're messy guys, all right. That's the only fun we get out of life—making a big mess, tearing everything up, and slopping around with this sticky stuff.'

'I say,' said Charles, but he didn't say anything. He turned and marched out.

He was unhappy for several days while the soundproof ceiling was installed.

Walking in the garden one day during the time this work was going on, I discovered a hidden plot of land, framed by high walls. Access to it was through a green door, usually locked. Now the door was open, and the workmen who installed the ceiling were whitewashing the inner walls of this retreat. I had always thought that it contained a kennel for Blue Blue, or that it was a kitchen garden. It was planted with grass, the same as the green grass carpet in front of the house, and in it were stuck two laundry poles sixteen feet apart. From the line strung between them hung Elsie's underclothes in privacy, drying in the sun. The laundry posts were painted like the boat-posts in Venice, with white and green stripes. Mother wanted everything in her world to be beautiful.

Mother hated cigar smoke and could detect its odour the next day. After dinner, when she left to go upstairs, we would take our cigars and retire to Charles's soundproofed room. We lit our cigars.

'Now we can talk as loud as we like,' said Charles… 'Don't drink that whisky like water—it'll make you liverish.'

Charles told me long stories there, of things he should publish as memoirs. We usually sat until four in the morning, and then I always walked up to bed on tiptoe. I was barely asleep one night when I heard a scream, and then some groans and moaning. It was Elsie's voice, loud and urgent. I put on my robe and ran to her room. I was certain she was being murdered. West was already with her when I arrived. Elsie looked like a wild bird that had come out of a fight with some fierce creature. She howled, she screamed like the seagulls, and in between she screeched like a cat.

'Mother is dying,' she said. 'For God's sake, don't stand around, do something!'

The maid who steadfastly refused to call Elsie 'milady' but was very efficient had brought a warm pad.

The doctor said on the phone that, instead of a hot-water bag, ice packs should be used, that it sounded like an appendix to him and he would be right over.

'Yeouww!' screamed Elsie. 'Mother is dying! Take my hand, Stevie.' I said that Mother was making too much noise for anybody dying.

The cook, Susan, came up. She was solidly built, round and good-natured. She wore a woollen bathrobe and felt slippers. 'Oh, milady,' she blubbered, 'oh, milady'—the tears were running over the round cheeks—'oh, milady...' She knelt and prayed.

Mother told Miss Bridget to make a fire. So far all this had taken place by the light of two candles. Suddenly Mother sat up and said, 'I wonder if anybody is trying to poison me?' And then she said, 'And where is my husband? Where is Sir Charles at a time like this?'

'He's asleep,' said the chauffeur, who, in pyjamas and bathrobe, had joined the group.

'Ah, ah! *Yeouww, yeouww!* Here are those knives again! Stevie, hold Mother's hand.' The ice pack came, and in the middle of her pain Mother said to the maid, 'Miss Bridget, will you put a scarf or something around that ice pack so it won't drip on this lovely fur blanket? *Yeouww, yeouww!* Where is the doctor, and for God's sake, will somebody wake up Sir Charles?'

Sir Charles came up, and he stopped in the door and asked, 'What seems to be the matter here?'

'I'm dying, that's all, and you ask what seems to be the matter! What's the matter with you? Didn't you hear me?'

'Well,' said Charles, 'it's that blasted ceiling you had put into my room, dear. It works both ways. You can't hear me, and I can't hear you.'

———

Next morning Mother was sitting in bed with a Schiaparelli turban on her head and wearing a jacket of green velvet on which a yellow wolf was embroidered. She was dictating to West. Holding up both her hands with the fingers spread, she turned to West. 'Now that my nails are dry, please call *Miss* Bridget.'

To me she said, 'Mother is going away for a while. Don't worry, she's not going to die, she's not going to make a fuss, and she doesn't want anyone else to make any fuss either!' She slapped her leg and kicked under the covers and let out the seagull cry. 'Ha!'

'Now we had a date with George Cukor for dinner tonight. I just sent a note. We shall do it the moment Mother gets back. He has a lovely house, and the food is very good there. By the way, Stevie, do you notice how busy all the servants are, and how happy? It's like when you leave a hotel and they're glad about the departure and waiting to get their tips.'

Bridget entered the room and said, 'And how are you this morning?'

Mother looked at her sharply. 'Don't ever ask me that again, *Miss* Bridget. God, how I hate personal questions! Don't ever ask me that again, or I shall tell you how I am. I shall tell you about the upper colon and the lower colon and the condition thereof, and also about the gall bladder, and my stomach. I shall describe all that to you in such vivid detail that you will be in the hospital instead of me.'

The maid ran out of the room, and Mother said, 'Ha! Talk about the servant problem! Now, Stevie, has Mother ever bored anyone with stories of her diseases or pains, except to say occasionally, "Damn all doctors"? I was brought up never to talk about my troubles. Anyway, while Mother is away, see that these terrible people make you comfortable. And now I'm ready to get up. I have a very busy day.'

I went below, where the departure was being organized. It was like the preparation for a transatlantic voyage.

'How is she? When is she leaving for the hospital?' Charles asked West.

'Oh, you know Lady Mendl, Sir Charles—*toujours la joie de vivre*. We're having twelve for lunch. What happens afterward I don't know. The doctor says he wants to operate tomorrow. Well, Lady Mendl doesn't choose to hear things like that.'

The chauffeur washed the Rolls-Royce, partly with his tears. Baskets of flowers, a portable picnic set with facilities for making cocktails, a case of bottles, the pillows with the famous mottoes, fur rugs, pictures, curtains—a truckload of stuff preceded the patient.

The doctor appeared after lunch and gave Elsie a sedative and then he talked a little about the hospital, the way one puts a patient at ease; he spoke about the latest equipment, the advances that had been made in the technique of administering anaesthesia, and he ended up his briefing with the statement that the hospital to which Mother was going was the most progressive. Mother, who had been dreaming about lovely things, and had sat there on the chaise longue with the polite smile she wore when not listening, picked up the last word of his speech. 'Progress!' she said. 'Listen, Doctor, you can keep your progress. Give me beauty!'

There were many things to settle. Susan the cook sniffled, and at last the haughty maid broke down and said, 'Milady, the lawyer is here.'

'What does he want?' Elsie sat up, and the lawyer and his clerk came in. They bowed, and the lawyer, who had come from San Francisco, mumbled something about the will; he thought it was advisable to go over it. Mother adjusted her skirt, and her face took on the Voltaire look. She waited until the servants were out of the room before she said, 'All right.' She took the paper and, biting off the words, began, '"To my beloved friend and secretary, Hilda West, I leave so and so much and this and that."

'"To my dear husband, Sir Charles Mendl, I leave this and that and so and so much." That also stays as it is.'

She continued with a list of beneficiaries and a bequest to everyone who had been in her service any length of time; to an old cook who lived in France, to two maids who were in Germany, to a butler in England, I leave this and that—and suddenly she became a little drowsy and seemed to fall asleep, but she woke up, and with the bad queen face she said angrily, 'And what do *I* get?'

The lawyer said, 'You get nothing, Lady Mendl.'

'Ha!' she yelled. 'Why don't I get anything?'

'Because you're dead and this is your last will and testament.'

She looked at the lawyer, still with the bad queen face, and she said, 'Do you play gin rummy?'

'Yes, I do,' said the lawyer.

Mother lost. The lawyer won sixteen dollars from her and was about to pocket his reward when she told him to go to a cabinet and bring from it a glass elephant. This beautiful transparent elephant had a small opening in its back, and it was stuffed with dollar bills. Mother held it towards the lawyer, and told him that it was for a very good cause, for anti-vivisection, and that he could contribute sixteen dollars.

The lawyer didn't want to play another game, and Charles sat down and lost twelve dollars. He handed them to Mother, saying, "'To him that hath shall be given.'"

She added, '"And from him that hath not shall be taken away even that which he hath." Don't quote the Scriptures to me, Charles. I know them.'

West came in and said that everything was ready now and that it was time to go.

The chauffeur dabbed at his eyes, and Susan whimpered, and Mother made the departure very cool and official. She drove off, waving her white-gloved hand as queens do. West stayed with her, and Charles came back alone.

He walked around the salon silently and went to his room; he didn't sing. He came out and walked in the garden. By cocktail time he had fixed his face and his phrases to suit the occasion. In a Foreign Office mood he issued the bulletins. He leaned back and said to all who approached him with concern, 'Poor darling, she's in the hospital, and that's the place where she'll be looked after properly.' The people left early.

Looking lost and years older, the jolly plum face now wrinkled, Charles said sadly, 'Let's go in to dinner.' The little green and white menu that always lay on the table was missing, the flowers were dead, the food indifferent, and the plates cold. The fire hadn't been lit and the curtains weren't drawn. The small lights that illuminated the cabinets were not on, the house was lonesome and neglected, the wind rattled an awning, and the palms were noisy outside. The moonlight threw the palms' swaying shadows against the wing in which Elsie's darkened apartment was.

Charles had to clear his throat before he spoke. With very tired voice and vacant eyes he said, 'She's really a fantastic

woman, you know. I'm very fond of her, and I hope she's fond
of me. I hope and pray that everything goes well. But if anything should happen, I should in that case take a small house,
with one servant—for, I assure you, this house will be haunted
by her ghost. In England there are ghosts everywhere. There
aren't any in new countries, but I believe that Elsie will start
the thing over here.'

'She's spent a good night and is in fine spirits,' was the bulletin.
Charles and I were at breakfast in the garden. The long telephone wires of Beverly Hills allow one to take the instrument
anywhere.

'I wonder,' said Charles, 'whether we should ask Hedy and
Nella for lunch, while Elsie is away.'

'Can't they come to the house when Mother is here?'

'Well, normally yes, but Hedy is one of those healthy girls
who shows that she is pregnant, and Elsie resents that. She
also resents—what's-her-name?—Nella, accepting invitations. She said, "I hate the women running around here with
an ambulance following them and the child almost popping
out." Now I don't mind it at all. I find women most beautiful
in that state. I'll call them.'

As he reached for the phone it rang. West was calling, and
she said to come to the hospital immediately. The doctor wanted
to have Sir Charles see what he could do to pacify Lady Mendl.
She had turned the whole hospital upside down and ignored
all the doctor's orders.

The cars were outside, Charles's and my own, but he said,
'It's quite a way out, miles from here. Let's use her essence, dear
boy. She can't use it and we're both low on coupons.'

Achille, with red-rimmed eyes, got some new flowers that had arrived, and we started off. We met West on the stairs of the hospital.

'Oh, she's difficult,' moaned West. 'Lady Mendl thinks this is a hotel. She made me hang printed signs on the doors of our rooms, "Do Not Disturb". She refuses to see anyone before eleven. She has unhinged the entire hospital. She kicked a nurse and she kicked a doctor in the stomach with her foot. The operation has been put off another day. The doctors are agreed that it's kidney stones, and there is a new way of operating on them. The technique is to crush the stones with pincers that reach into the bladder without opening the patient. The crushed stones then leave with the urine.'

The hospital was staffed by very young and very old nurses, and we went up in the peculiar elevators of hospitals that accommodate the wagons on which people are wheeled into operating rooms. We came out and saw the curious signs, green and white decorated with the wolf, saying: 'Do Not Disturb'.

The chauffeur had moist eyes again. At the door of the room Charles said, 'Achille, you go in first with the flowers.'

It was noon. We heard Elsie's voice.

'This is no hour to visit anybody in a hospital, Achille. Don't you know any better? Go outside and come back later, and, for heaven's sake, stop crying.'

Charles and I went in.

'I said to West to tell people to come in the late afternoon, that's when one wants to see visitors, not in the morning, Charles.'

'Well, I came because the doctor seems worried, Elsie dear.'

'Ha!' cried Elsie. 'Don't talk to me about doctors or nurses!'

'If we came too early, I'm sorry, darling, we'll leave.'

'No, since you're here, stay. Oh, the things that have happened to me in this place that calls itself a hospital!'

Mother was sitting up in bed, in white, and surrounded by as many beautiful objects as could be placed in a room that was square and mainly occupied by a bed. There were pictures on the wall, many vases of flowers, and the portable wicker bar for visitors.

'The things they are doing here are perfectly awful,' said Mother, making the worst bad queen face and hitting the side of the bed. 'Three so-called nurses do things to me—perfectly indecent things—and I have to lie here and take it. Imagine!' She picked up a bath towel. 'You see this, Charles? Feel it, and imagine taking the most tender part of your anatomy and rubbing and scrubbing and rubbing some more, first with warm water, then with cold. When the one with the cold water came, that's when I lost patience and kicked her.'

She glowered at Charles. 'They come in here and wake you up, and then they bring breakfast at daybreak, and then comes that bath in bed. Then they make the bed while you're in it, and then come the doctors and poke around my insides. And this Viennese specialist that is so highly regarded, he seems to bring people in from off the streets—anybody at all who wants to have a look at me, as long as they call themselves "Doctor"— that seems to be all the identification they need—and I call it disgusting! Why don't they look at the pictures of my insides which they took all day yesterday? I can't wait to get out of here, and to take the first plane or boat to France.'

West came and said that the head of the hospital was coming to talk to Mother. Mother felt better. She pounded a pillow and sat up. 'I'll tell him a thing or two about hospitals,' she said, 'and the way they treat people when they're helpless. And I'm not going to have another bath or let anyone come in here to inspect me. I refuse to submit to any more obscenity. Make a sign, West, that says: "No Visitors, Please".'

We left. The parting was cool.

In the car Charles said, 'Poor darling—you know, Bernard Shaw objected to the same thing. He said one doesn't wash antiques. Fancy this happening to poor Elsie. For once, beauty is not her shield.'

Later, on La Brea Avenue, he said, 'Poor Elsie is worried about the cost of the operation. She's afraid it will cut into the funds set aside for the restoration of Versailles—she worries about that a great deal. But I'm glad the old girl looked well, not at all like someone who is about to die.'

West called later and said that the head of the hospital had come to see Lady Mendl.

'Did he give her a good talking to?' asked Charles.

'No. She persuaded him to let her redecorate the floor we are on, "to make it look civilized"—those were her ladyship's own words.'

10

The Little Red Clock

Mother was back from the hospital. She was up early and out on her small balcony. It was only ten, and she had already had her frugal breakfast and was doing her eye exercises. The California sun is so bright that I wore sunglasses walking in the garden. She called to me.

Mother's legs were covered by her best fur rug, and in the process of waving sunlight into her eyes, she said to me, 'You'll spoil your sight, Stevie, wearing those sunglasses. Take them off and do as I do, and you'll never need glasses. Only creatures of darkness are blind—moles, worms, and fishes deep down, and such.'

The next step in her exercises was to place the palms of her hands crossed over her eyes, resting the elbows on a green pillow. This, called palming, is done for a few minutes; and after that, a paddle, such as is used to play ping-pong, which is painted white and on which black dots appear, is moved close to the eyes and then away from them. The last routine is to stand up and do what is called the Elephant Swing.

You stand relaxed—the way elephants do when they stand and swing back and forth—then you swing to the left and to the right, slowly, the eyes moving, so that they move with the body. You start at an object on the left—in this case it was the roof of the adjoining house. From there you followed the upper edge of a wall, then the lower line of the tiles on the roof of an outhouse, until you came to the end. From this point you went back again, over the tiles, over the wall, to the roof of the adjoining house. This was done twenty times. I joined the eye exercises.

Finally Mother called a halt to this and Bridget put away the magnifying glass. Mother closed her eyes and reclined on the sofa. West came out on the terrace and sat down. It was still the lovely California morning. Birds were on the lawn, and the gardener was up in one of the palm trees, removing the dried leaf that had scraped against the white wall the day Mother had left for the hospital. The hospital was not mentioned. Elsie was completely repaired. She smiled the little girl smile, she took off the white gloves that had become slightly soiled during the exercises and put on a new snow-white pair.

Then she leaned back and said with closed eyes, 'Mother is going to tell you the life story of a little girl—called Elsie. Don't be afraid. We're not going to go into childhood.' She made the bad queen face. 'Oh, how Mother can do without that, as far as memories go! We will remember only the wonderful moments. Stevie dear, you know, when I count I still have to use my fingers, and when I had my great success in New York, naturally I had to have somebody to write down figures, and that man wrote everything into a ledger, and when there was a profit he wrote it down in black ink. So I told him—how silly—when there was anything to the good, I wanted to see it immediately, it had to stand out, and I wanted to have it written in red ink. Well, the poor man was very confused, he couldn't understand that at all. Anyway, that's the way I ran my business. Now, don't you wonder how it was possible for me to get anywhere with methods like that? How *was* it possible? I ask myself sometimes.' Mother cast a glance at me and smiled sweetly.

West said, 'It was because Lady Mendl had Price Waterhouse and Company go over the books every two weeks.'

Mother shot a deadly look at West, then folded her hands again. 'They were all good friends of Mother's—Price Waterhouse, and dear Mr Frick, and dear Stanford White— and they wanted to help Mother. In this life, Stevie, as I have told you before, one must have good friends—that's most important. Now, Mother had good friends. I had very little money when I started, but I was very rich in friends, and every one of them was going to give me from ten thousand dollars up to a hundred thousand, and then I was to open a business.

'But before I was ready, my beloved friend Stanford White, the great architect of that time, gave me the order to decorate the Colony Club. It was my first order, and for fifty thousand dollars—correct me if I'm wrong, West, you have such a good memory for detail—and I thanked all my good friends, Miss Anne Morgan and Mrs Vanderbilt and Elisabeth Marbury, I thanked them all, and I told them that I did not need their money, for a great architect had put his faith in me and given me carte blanche. That's also most important—for people to have faith in you. Well, the rest is history. I opened the doors of the American house, and the windows, and let in the air and the sunshine. Up to then everything was closed, and people never used what they called the parlour in their houses, and the furniture was sentimental and gloomy, and doom hung in the rooms where it stood. I think I may say that I created the profession of interior decorator. I may also say that I rescued the American house and made it liveable. I wasn't perfect at the beginning. I made mistakes. I thought for a while that yellow was a colour, and after I saw Rome I convinced myself that beige—the colour of that city—was a colour. I am not speaking of painting, I mean a colour for the interiors of houses. I picked, however, good shades of it. I did other things I wouldn't do today—I used Chinese wallpapers, flowered cretonnes, frilled lampshades, and taffeta ruching. I believed in these things for a while. I threw them out as time went on.

'Louis Quatorze, Louis Quinze and Seize, became my loves. I am accused of having made America conscious of antiques. Mr Robsjohn-Gibbings has stated that this is a dubious honour and that I have retarded modern trends. Well, to this I say that good antiques live very happily with modern things, and especially against modern backgrounds. This is not a lecture on furniture, Stevie. I'll tell you about that another time. I just wanted to tell you how I got my start, which is the hardest part in life. After the Colony Club I received commissions to decorate women's clubs all over America, and they were all done carte blanche—and I became famous and made a fortune. Private clients followed. It happened almost over-night—commissions and money rolled in from Mrs William Crocker of San Francisco, Ogden Armour of Lake Forest; I did the Weyerhaeuser house in Minneapolis, and then Mr Henry Frick's in New York. I made fewer and fewer mistakes as time went on.'

Mother was a little tired. She said, 'You know, Stevie, why Mother did all that? Not to make money for its own sake—I have kept little enough of that. I did it only to buy beautiful things, and one day to be able to buy the most beautiful house in the world, and to have it for myself, and to entertain therein, so perfectly, so beautifully. To lavish on that house all the infinite care that a house wants, that anything in this world which you love deserves. I can't paint, I can't write, I can't sing, but I can decorate and run a house, and light it, and heat it, and have it like a living thing, and so right that it will be the envy of the world, the standard of perfect hospitality.' Elsie banged on the table. 'Just wait until you see Versailles. One day soon we'll go—to my perfect Eden. West, have we any news from my beloved Versailles?'

'A stack of bills, Lady Mendl.'

'What's the matter with you today, West? Get back aboard the future—' Mother turned to me. '"The future", Stevie, is a beautiful balloon, with a golden gondola, in which Mother sails through the clouds.'

West reached for a basket of letters and telegrams. 'It's settled about Wasserman Negative, Illegitimate Jones,' she said, handing a cable to Mother.

Mother explained to me that 'Wasserman negative, illegitimate Jones' was written on a card at the head of a hospital bed and identified a little coloured baby that had been fathered by an American soldier in France.

That evening, as West was feeding her cats under the eucalyptus tree, she said that Mother didn't like to talk about the good deeds she performed. 'Think of it—at her age, to adopt a brood of children and to provide for their education until they are grown up. It would be a problem with normal children, but Lady Mendl has complicated it. She says, "Anybody can adopt pretty boys and girls. I want to have the ugly, the ones with birthmarks, the troubled ones. I want to have children with spirit rather than beauty." And so we have waiting for us in Versailles this kindergarten of sad little French boys and girls and now also an American—Wasserman Negative, Illegitimate Jones. Lady Mendl is a remarkable woman.

'Did you know that in the First World War she was in the Battle of the Marne, all the way up front, in the Chemin des Dames, as nurse, in uniform? And the Germans were bombarding Compiègne and she refused to leave until all her wounded were evacuated, and then she didn't go, and did a typical Lady Mendl thing. In the basement of the house in which they spent most of the time, on account of the heavy shelling, she remembered that a few cans of petrol had been left. She did not want these to fall into the hands of the Germans. Anybody else would have spilled out the petrol and set it on fire. But Lady Mendl got someone to help her and buried the cans, and she made a sketch of the place and put a broken wheelbarrow there to mark the spot. All this under fire. Finally they put her on one of the last ambulances and made her leave. The tide of battle turned after that and she went back, and they were still there, the cans of petrol.'

West collected her kitty cats and puthy cats to put them to bed.

It was again the quiet hour, when the first violet light of the California evening invaded the garden, when all was still and only the small evening sounds of the birds, a kind of muted chatter, were heard.

Mother was smiling and happy, and with good right. Everybody else living has, at one time or other, the unpleasant task of making out a cheque to a hospital: Mother was different—she sent them a bill. She sat at her well-lighted, orderly desk and, with green ink in a bold hand, calculated the value of her services while there. She had done a very much needed job.

'Again I was up against the unspeakables,' she said. 'The amount of hideous functional things is greater in a hospital than anywhere else. That is really a place for a designer. And also, they might use a little more imagination in naming these places.' For instance, that big hospital—what's its name? the Cedars of Lebanon—sounds as if you were going to a cemetery.'

The bill was all made up and Mother handed it to West to type. Mother called the butler and asked for the time, and then she looked at the little red clock. 'Did Mother ever tell you the story of that little red clock, Stevie?'

Mother hadn't.

'Sit down here, and Mother will tell you about a mistake she made.

'As Mother advanced in the business of decorating, she made fewer and fewer mistakes. That, of course, is the consequence of applying oneself and keeping in mind the three cardinal principles which I have told you about, Simplicity, Suitability, and Proportion. Well, this dear clock, which in itself had all these qualities, was a mistake.

'One day, my dear friend Mr Frick—who was an ideal client and a gentleman, and besides, a man of good taste—called Mother. He collected pictures, the best of them. There are among that class of people many who collect things, but the only thing they're really good at is collecting money. In art they collect the second-best stuff of the good painters and all the best of the third-rate artists—and I suppose that is, in a way, as it should be, for if there weren't any second-rate pictures there wouldn't be any first-rate ones.

'At any rate, Mr Frick was so well advised that his house now is a first-rate museum, and the pictures share the rooms with the furniture Mother bought. He called me, and what a wonderful thing it is to be given a free hand to buy anything, to be told that price was of no importance, that quality only mattered. I set forth and went to France, and when something exceedingly good, and in consequence very costly, came to my attention, I did not buy it on the spot, but I wrote down a careful description of it and had it photographed and sketched, and sent all this information to Mr Frick. And in every case he said to go ahead.

'And so one day Mother came across that dear little clock— the smallest clock to strike the hours in clear tones. I fell in love with it immediately. I took it back to America myself.

'The furniture was placed in the rooms of that great house on Fifth Avenue, and Mr Frick was very happy with it. "You have done a perfect job," he said to me, and then he asked whether I was satisfied, and I said that in general I was satisfied and thought that I had carried out my assignment.

'"There is only one mistake I made," I said to Mr Frick.

'"And what is that?"

'I led him to the room on the mantel of which stood the little red clock.

'"What's wrong with it?" he asked.

'I said that I had violated my own dictates, for while the little red clock in itself had Simplicity, Proportion, and Suitability, the proportions of the room were such that the little clock was out of proportion.

'And that dear Mr Frick said, "Well, if that is all that's wrong, dear Elsie, don't let that worry you." He went to the mantel and took the little red clock and handed it to me. "It's yours, a gift from me, in gratitude for getting me all these beautiful things." And that is how Mother got the little red clock that accompanies Mother wherever she goes.

'Those clients, Stevie, are getting fewer and fewer.'

11

The Prospect of Tara

West was sitting under the well-groomed eucalyptus tree, with her six kitty cats and puthy
cats, feeding them from the breakfast tray,
which the second man had brought out. Coombs paid attention
to West only when she was at table with the family. Now she
was comforting a red and white cat, striped like a tiger.

'If I ever found myself alone in a room with him I'd lock
the door and throw the key out of the window, and then I'd
turn myself into a tigress and I'd go for him. I'd bite and claw
him until he was dead.'

'We know who you mean, West. What's he done now?'
asked Charles.

'When my puthy cats were little kittens he persuaded Lady
Mendl not to allow them to stay in the house. This morning
he found Midgy here, she was in the kitchen, because Susan
likes her, and he kicked her with the tip of his boot, so that the
poor puthy cat flew into the screen door. And then he chased
her out through the back of the house and threw a flowerpot
after her. The pieces are still there in the garage—you can go
and look at them there, Sir Charles.'

'Well, it's no use saying anything to Elsie about it. That would only make it worse.'

'Well, am I to take this just like that, without saying a word, Sir Charles?'

'There are ways of getting back at him, West.'

'If you think of anything, Sir Charles, let me know.'

The second man came out and said to West, 'Lady Mendl wants to see you in her bathroom. She wants to dictate.'

'When I write the story of my life,' said West, 'it's going to be called "Thirty-two Years in Lady Mendl's Bathroom".'

West kissed the injured puthy cat and put it down, and with a saucer of milk from her breakfast she walked to the garage, where the cats lived. After that she marched resolutely back to the house and slammed the door as she went in.

'Faithful and strong as a horse,' said Charles. 'Comes from Norwegian stock. Still, I don't know how she stands it, day after day, year in, year out.

'I'm afraid we're going into a heavy sea. Elsie is about to do a house, prepare yourself. Come with me and we'll have a look at it. It's right up the canyon.

'They made a picture here called *Gone with the Wind*, and in this was a house, called Tara, and this house fascinated so many people here that you see copies of it all over, small Taras and big ones. Houses grow here overnight. Sometimes when I take a walk and pass a place that was a potato field last time, it has become Tara Number Ten, with moss on old trees and white-haired darky retainers. They carry on outside their studios the way they do inside. Ah, here is the Prospect of Tara. That's the way Elsie names her productions. She letters it on a white folder in her bold hand, with green ink: "Prospect of

Versailles" or "Prospect of This-and-That", and this morning in her bathroom I saw "Prospect of Tara". That's when I knew that we were going to have heavy weather, dear boy.'

This Tara was the largest edition of all—well proportioned, surrounded by terraced gardens, flanked by old oak trees, which, Sir Charles explained, one buys at a nursery called Personality Trees, Inc.

The house seemed in good condition. There was a For Sale sign on it, in the style of the house, giving the name of the broker. At the gate was an immense mailbox, a replica of Tara in miniature.

'Let's not go in. That's the car of La Flèche at the door. The housefly is in there, busy making plans.'

When we came back home Coombs said to me, 'Lady Mendl wishes to see you in her bathroom.'

Elsie's bathroom was her private salon and office. The bath itself was a small marble pool, into which water ran from the beaks of two silver swans. The walls were vast panes of faded mirrors. One corner was taken up by a low banquette uphol-stered in dark green with white piping. The floor was covered with a material resembling the pelt of shaggy, snow-white goats. There was a small dresser with photographs in silver frames, a beautiful ormolu clock with alabaster columns.

Everything in the room was costly and in good taste. The proportions were perfect, and there was, of course, no 'unspeak-able', not even a basin in which to wash one's hands. There were long-stemmed lilies close to the bath, with many of their leaves. Elsie had taken on a new personality. She was alabaster, in white gloves, silken turban, and she wore the wolf jacket; over her legs was what she called Mother's best fur blanket, a satin-lined vicuña coverlet, light and warm. She looked like the engravings one finds in the histories of war and of German armies, like the very old German generals of the time of Frederick the Great.

'Sit down, Stevie.' She turned her face upward and produced the face of a martyr at the highest moment of ecstasy. She did all her shenanigans of joy—kicking up her feet under the coverlet, making *chk-chk*, and she let out the old seagull cry, 'Ha!' She said, 'Come closer to Mother, Stevie, and let Mother tell you about something marvellous that has happened.

'There's a house for sale. It's on Benedict Canyon Drive.' She took up the folder marked 'Prospect of Tara'. 'Now Mother doesn't know anything about money, or stocks and bonds, or any other kind of business. But she knows houses. Now this house is perfect inside and out. The garden is in order, the rooms are in first-rate shape. Mother won't have to spend a cent on it. The property is being sold to close an estate, and it's in escrow or something like that—anyway, documentary terms that Mother doesn't understand are involved. It's for sale at a ridiculous price. Now Mother has several clients who want a house out here. Here, for example, is a letter from Evalyn Walsh MacLean, who writes: "I want a house desperately. I can't find one, and I give you a blank cheque. Buy a house for me and furnish it. Anything you think is OK is OK with me." She wants that house six months from now.

'Here is another letter from the Baronne de Winter: "I need a house, as soon as you can find one, for four months. Not too large, four master bedrooms, etc. I will bring my own staff." Now, listen to Mother. She has a lot of beautiful things pining away in storage. The rest she will buy. I'll furnish the house and rent it to the baronne first, and then sell it to Evalyn, and in the process double my money. After that we'll go to Versailles— *chk-chk*. And then Mother will at last be able to do the things she's always wanted to do, without worrying about the cost.'

She banged on the floor with the Prospect of Tara. The daybed on which she sat was very low, but the fur covering did not give any emphasis to the Prospect being banged; so she banged it on the cover of a large book on furniture that was beside her.

'Now, the first thing Mother is going to do is to get rid of two little houses she owns. When Mother came here, people in California were afraid that the Japanese would land on this coast, and every thing was for sale dirt cheap; and Mother bought two little houses and furnished them, and she's going to sell them now, and with that money buy the big house and furnish it.'

Monsieur La Flèche came in, with plans under his arm, and suddenly I did not exist any longer. I left the room.

Mother had a terrible day the next day. She slapped her knee and then spoke to an invisible man who stood somewhere in the room, before the sofa on which we were seated and to the right of her. When she needed money for one of her causes, her face and voice changed, her jaw came forward, and she banged on tables and furniture.

'There he was, that awful man—oh, it was perfectly awful, Stevie! He said, "You can't sell the house." Now what do you think about that? He talked party of the first part, party of the second part, and this and that awful thing, and words like escrow, and other words equally unsympathetic, and Mother said to him, "Listen, Mr What's-your-name, Mr Read and Write and whatever or whatever your name is—'" She shook her finger at the invisible man. 'I said to him, "Get it down, do whatever you have to do, and do it quickly, because, to be frank, I don't enjoy being here, I hate banks. So do it very quickly, and if that is the law of California that you are quoting to me, I'm glad I'm leaving soon."

'You see, Stevie, these wild asses from the prairies sit there, and they think I'm an old woman. I'll teach them! I'll buy them and sell them before they get up out of their swivel chairs.

'There are two houses, and I am the rightful owner. I have a customer who wants to buy both houses, lock, stock and barrel. For one he will pay thirty thousand; and for the other, twenty-five. That's fifty-five thousand for both, which will go a long way toward buying Tara.

'Now this Mr Swivel Chair folds his hands as if he were going to say a prayer. He has a mouth full of bad teeth, and a speech defect, oh, "gouh goom—gum" he goes, and I have to listen to him carefully to hear the nonsense he is talking. "You cannot sell a property," he says, "according to the law of the State of California, for double what you paid for it, as recently as that." So I said to him, "Listen, do you know the value of a Whistler drawing? Have you any idea of a toile needlework seat on a Directoire chair? Do you know the value of a small Aubusson carpet, six by eight? Of course you don't!" He looked at me with his fish eyes, and kept his eyes on my face and his hands locked, and then he picked up the contract and looked at it.

'So I told him. I said, "Listen to me, Mr Read and Write, perhaps I bought them cheaply, but into these houses went thousands of dollars of money, in work, construction, and furnishings, and that is all calculated here to the last cent. Now, look here, you don't want me to give them away. I am selling them at a low figure as it is," I said, "*cheap*, for if we charged for my direction—I visited these houses constantly while the work was in progress—then, Mr Bank of America, then I should demand a hundred thousand dollars apiece for them, and not twenty-five and thirty.

"'And probably get it," said the Swivel Chair. And I said, "Not probably, but certainly get it."

'Oh, Stevie, and I had to have the cleaners in, and all the furniture had to be done over, and the carpets cleaned. These awful people that had the one house—what's the name, a Communist screenwriter, I am told, and his frightful bride—stains everywhere, and rings from glasses. There must have been a lot of drinking going on in that house! Oh, Stevie, I had a terrible day, and when I saw that furniture I thought of Versailles, and those awful Germans that were there for four long years—or was it three? And then our own soldiers, which is probably worse. The Germans at least have a sense of order. I'm not so afraid of the British or the French. But ours, they can be awful rough on furniture.

'But we shall hear all about that, Stevie. Tonight a general, a British liaison officer, is coming to dinner, and he wrote me a note saying that he had been out to Versailles and had been to the Villa Trianon.'

In due course the general appeared. He was the very image of a British liaison officer, handsome, tall, the Foreign Office type, in faultless uniform. Everything on him was right—our men look like airline pilots next to the British. They hold on to glory in the liveries of their officers and lackeys alike.

'*Chk-chk,*' said Mother when he came in the door. There were people who outranked him at the party, but on account of his having visited Versailles, he was placed at Elsie's right. At her left sat a Scottish lord.

Mother smoothed her skirt and made the little girl face, then braced her chin and looked at the general with pleading eyes. 'Tell me, General, how did you find my dear Villa Trianon? What have the Germans left of it?'

'Oh, it's there,' said the general, 'in good condition.'

'Oh,' said Mother, 'do you know anything about the condition of a house and about furniture?'

He said 'Yes', but Mother said, 'If you did, you wouldn't be a good general, and you are a good general, I hope. But never mind that. Close your eyes, General.' She took his hand and squeezed it hard. 'Keep your eyes closed and, in your military fashion, walk into the villa and tell me what you saw.'

'Well, downstairs in the hall were several Secret Service men and two motor cycles.'

'Oh Lord!' said Mother. 'Stop right there. You're breaking my heart!' She closed her eyes, and after a pause she said weakly, 'Let's walk into the dining-room. What did you find there?'

'In the dining-room was a large table with charts, and at that table sat Lord Gort, Air Marshal Tedder, General Lefèvre, and an aide-de-camp.'

'The furniture, the furniture, General! What chairs did you see? They all sat on chairs, didn't they?'

'Yes, they sat on chairs, Lady Mendl.'

'What kind of chairs?'

'I couldn't see, they were sitting on them.'

'Did you have a chance to see anything? Did you just go in and out, or did you stay any length of time, General? Did you observe anything at all except things military like the motor cycles and air marshals?'

The general said, 'Let me see, I arrived at 13:30, and I stayed until the next morning—02—I left precisely at 02—driving back to Paris.'

'Go on! Close your eyes again, and never mind the chairs or the correct time. Let's go upstairs, or didn't you go upstairs. You had to go upstairs if you stayed there a whole evening, as you just told me. Come, come, close your eyes again, General. Now we're going up the stairs. Was there a carpet on them?'

'I don't remember, I really can't recall.'

'Well, that's most probably gone. Oh, dear Lord, there was the most beautiful pink and black flowered Ispahan, cut up. Nobody ever cut up an Ispahan carpet before I did, and put it on a staircase. Go on, we're upstairs now—was there any furniture at all upstairs?'

'Oh, I remember,' said the general, 'upstairs were some beds.'

'What kind of beds?'

'Oh, beds—oh yes, I remember now, I lay down on one for a while. French furniture. It looked like a room in a bordello.'

'Well,' Mother said sharply. 'Sir, I have never been in a bordello—I thank you, but I know what you mean. Go on—what was on the walls?'

'There were some awful drawings on pale paper, I think; yellowish paper, now that I think of it. I spent quite a while in that room, it comes back to me.'

'Go on, General—'

'These drawings were in large red and gold frames.'

'Oh, thank God! Those are my famous Drian drawings.'

He said, 'I'm sorry.'

Mother said, 'Thank you, General, you've made me very happy. You can open your eyes now, General. Remember what I told you at the beginning of our talk. I said you couldn't be a good general if you knew anything about furniture. Well, you are a very good general, I am sure. What you took for a bed in a bordello was my dear, dear Louis Fourteenth bed.'

She kicked the general in the ribs and disarranged his composure for a second. He pulled his tunic straight, straightened out his moustache, pulled Elsie's chair, and walked with her to the salon. Then he fled to the side of Sir Charles, where he remained for the rest of the evening.

When we were alone Mother said to me, 'Isn't it curious that a man so interesting-looking, so handsome, can be so simple? Is it because he is a general?'

I told Mother about an old French saying, which goes: 'Why are generals so stupid? Because they are picked from among the colonels.'

12

Central Casting

It was very unusual to see Charles in the upper part of the house. He came into my room early one morning, and he seemed agitated. He had no car, and he had to go to the RKO lot—would I take him? '*Die alte Frau*—' he began. When Charles called Elsie *die alte Frau* instead of 'old girl', it was always on account of some great annoyance. He switched automatically to German then, in case any servants were within earshot.

'Do you know what *die alte Frau* has done to me now? She has sold me to the movies! Well, she did it over coffee the other night, not only for me but also for Count Bobino, at whose house we were dining. She leaned against Cheever Cowdin, and both looked across the table at me, and she said, "Look at jolly old England. Now, why don't you have Charles play himself in a film?" As simple as that. And then she looked at Bobino and said, "Now, there's nobody looks so much like a French count as Bobino. Why don't you have a real one play that part instead of hiring somebody like Boyer?" Well, Cheever must have told someone, for Hitchcock called. They're making a picture with Ingrid Bergman and Cary Grant, and I shall be in it, and so will Bobino. So imagine. We had to be there with the daylight, first at a place called Central Casting, and then at some government place, and sign papers, and someone called out, "Sir Charles Mendl", and "Count Bobino", and they said, "Here is your Social Security card for your unemployment insurance." So now I'm in it. I'm labour—I even had to join a union.

'I suppose Elsie will ask ten-per-cent commission from each of us. Now, I don't mind, but Bobino has been trying to act for years. He has entertained producers and directors at his house for months in the hope of getting a part in a picture. He has fed them all the specialities of his house and cooked his fine soups for them, made dishes of the high kitchen, sent them away with packets of butter, lobsters, and boxes of snails. But they all discouraged him; they said, "What do you want to be a lousy actor for?" Finally he has made it. Thanks to Elsie, we shall be in the same film together.'

Everybody prophesied a great future on the screen for Charles, and in a few days he had puffed himself into Churchillian Britishness. He pronounced everything the way a telephone operator does numbers. He walked about wearing the mantle of empire, and he spoke of his career at luncheon, cocktails, and dinner.

The film started and the tests were made, and finally the day came when Charles was to play the part of an elderly playboy who entered a ship's cabin by mistake. They had requested Charles to be there by seven, and he had been in make-up for hours. I went to visit him on the set, to watch the takes. Although he had all the correct clothes required, a special yachting costume had been designed for him. They had accented the jolliness. Charles sat in Ingrid's dressing-room, waiting. Bobino walked about with arms crossed and biting his lip. He had been cast as a butler.

Charles had a piece of paper in his hand with about thirty words on it, which he read several times, and then he asked Ingrid to rehearse him. She told him he was perfect.

The moment finally came. At first Charles said his lines quite naturally, but afterwards, in the confusion of the set, the many directions, the heat and glare of the lights, he ran up on them, and Hitchcock finally decided that Charles should say something that came naturally to him. He asked me for a suggestion. The script demanded that Charles walk into the wrong cabin, in which sat a beautiful woman, Ingrid Bergman, and upon seeing her he was to say something. I suggested that he exclaim, 'What a ravishing creature!'—a phrase that came naturally to him. They had to take the scene over and over, because now poor Charles suffered from stage fright. Finally they wrote the speech on a blackboard, and a man held it up for Charles to read.

Hitchcock said again, 'Ready—lights—camera' and Charles opened the door and came in. He looked, pulled his pince-nez from his waistcoat pocket, and read off the board, 'I say—ah—what a ravishing creature!' Hitchcock was enchanted. 'Perfect!' he said. 'Cut!' And that was the end of Charles's work at the studio. The bit was left in the film and is very amusing.

Less fortunate was Bobino. He found himself playing a butler. Butlers in movies are very important, but, as a butler, he could not wear his monocle. Without the monocle he was blind, and the scenes took a very long time. They had to take them over and over because he walked past the stand with the champagne bucket, knocking it over, and then reached for the flowers on the table, or the candlestick, instead of the bottle. He finally learned to do it blindly. He bowed correctly, smiled, pulled the bottle from the ice, and opened it. During this business there was a long piece of dialogue between Cary Grant and Ingrid Bergman.

The director was not satisfied with the script. He changed the lines and had the scene taken over several times. The patient professionals did it again and again, but the amateur Bobino wilted. He had opened close to forty bottles of champagne without seeing them. He said that his fingers hurt, and after five more takes he was completely through and was replaced.

'I have enough. What a terrible way to make a living!' said Bobino.

'I am very happy,' said Sir Charles. 'I am being paid a thousand a week, and the contract is for ten weeks.'

Count Bobino put his monocle back and went to the infirmary to have something done about his fingers. Charles waved and smiled at several ravishing creatures that passed.

When we were in the car he said, 'Now, ten times a thousand, that makes ten thousand. I thought I'd give that to Elsie towards her project. She's a little short of cash. She knows nothing whatever about life in general, but houses and furniture she knows, and I trust her blindly. This will give me a great puff with her, and what's even better, we'll make money on it. I'd like to have put in more. Now, if they'd have let me sing in this picture, that would have been another matter. Then I could have easily contributed a hundred thousand.'

While we were driving home Charles said, 'As soon as it got around that I was to be an actor, that bad hat Halvah came around. I'm told he's a good agent, and he said he'd like to put me on the radio. He has an idea about a programme. I'd come out of our house, stroll in the garden, and sing, and that would pay very well. Then I might persuade Elsie to give up this silly idea of going to Versailles, and we could stay on here. Or else I'd have a good excuse not to go, except for a short time, for my work would keep me here. Elsie might go to Versailles alone and come back here in the autumn.

'Now I can't understand Elsie at all. There's that fellow she won't have at the house, the Empty Stomach, as she calls him. He, Munchin, is building vast housing developments, Munchinville and Munchintown, whatever he calls them, and he has said to me that if Elsie would create an interior for one of them, it would be known by her name and copied thousands of times, and each time Elsie would get a royalty, and that would amount to a fortune. I told her, and she was livid. She started a tirade against the enemies of beauty; she said she did not want to design anything that went into a house that was like a thousand others. She went on for hours. *Gott im Himmel! Die alte Frau* can be very trying if you get into the furniture department with her.

'The things she's done to me! She's put me in this sound-conditioned room, which is not big enough to swing a cat in, and now she's letting me make a bloody fool of myself acting on the screen. It's from the sublime to the gor blymie! That, dear boy, is a cockney expression and means "God bless me!"'

Charles told Achille to drive home the pretty way, which took so long that when we arrived at Benedict Canyon we saw Bobino, in his garden, busy with his snail trees. He lifted his bandaged hand and waved with it.

13

The Anniversary

Mother was in the small salon playing cards and, as usual, relieving Atwater Kent of some money. It went into the glass elephant when he won. The glass elephant was now working for the little children of Versailles, and Atti was gladly losing large sums of stuff into the crystal poor box.

Charles reported on the happenings of the day and his experiences on Stage Eight, and after Mr Kent had gone he said to Mother that he would invest in her enterprise to his limit. Mother made *chk-chk* and gave him a grateful look with her little girl face.

Suddenly she became serious and asked for the folder on the Prospect of Tara. Holding up a bridge pad on which she made calculations, she said that unfortunately we were still in what she called the black and that a little more money had to come forth—not much, but something. She looked from face to face, like an auctioneer, but there were no bids, and so she slammed the prospectus closed and got up.

She staggered two paces and then stood stiffly still. Turning to Charles, she said darkly, with the bad queen face, 'Tonight is our anniversary, in case you have forgotten, Charles. We're being given a party by the Korniloffs, and I'm ordering the car for seven.'

'Dammit,' said Charles in the corridor, 'I wonder who reminded the old girl. I thought she'd forgotten. She forgot last year. It must be West; she loves parties as much as Elsie, but dislikes to do the work on them, so she gets other people to give them. Now the Korniloffs are charming people—always champagne and caviar on ice there. That's a regime I'm not opposed to. I think it's the perfect diet for longevity—caviar, the grey-green slimy kind in the big blue cans, from Grosrybrest; we might get some of that tonight. It's very hard to come by these days; if anyone can get it, it's Sascha Korniloff.'

Mother said later, 'Money, money, money! All we need now, Stevie, is around a thousand dollars.'

The collection of this money was like the financing of a Broadway musical comedy which everybody knew was going to be a smash hit. The money was needed, but the privilege of investing was limited to certain people. We had all subscribed to our limit already. And none was wanted from a bank or an outsider.

'The car, milady,' said Coombs.

The Korniloffs were also party lovers, and they were enshrined on one of the hills of Hollywood, a vast hill all to themselves. The relationship between husband and wife in that household was very pleasant. Mama had all the money, and Sascha Korniloff, the energy and love of life; he was like a samovar, warm and expansive.

Although he was a Georgian he did not call himself a prince. He loved cars and pretty girls, in that order, and he was so warm of heart that when he saw any one of his friends he mangled him with affection. He greeted the arriving guests, usually at the top of the stairs of his house, with a loud fanfare of his deep voice. Then he held his arms away from his body and, as if attempting to fly, descended the steps; meanwhile his blue eyes filled with tears; and, when he finally was at the bottom, he embraced the friends, squeezing the air out of them. Then came the handshake and the pat on the back, all perfectly sincere, and many people wished he liked them less as they gasped and rearranged their clothes. He spoke as Russians of that region do, as if he had a stone in his mouth, and when he pronounced double 'l' as in 'all' or 'well', the stone seemed to roll forward; the vowel sounded hollow and large, and he seemed to inject a 'w' and an 'o' after it. 'All' sounded like 'Awoll'.

It was said that he had the prowess of Casanova, and there were stories of Arabian nights that he had arranged. He was, however, extremely discreet in a town of talkers. His eyes, even when he was not drunk, looked as if they were under two magnifying glasses, and he had the directness and honesty of primitive people. His wife and he were sitting with me one time at Romanoff's, and at the next table sat a ravishing creature. He wanted to know her name, and I introduced him. She was with an actor. 'You are the most peuwtifoowl thing what I have ever seen,' said Korniloff. 'What's your telephone number?' The girl laughed and gave it to him.

Korniloff, who was far-sighted, said to his wife, 'Mama, the glasses.' Madame Korniloff took off her glasses, and he put them on and wrote down the number, and then got up and went over and said to the girl, 'Have I got it right?'

He never spoke to the man. He returned the glasses to Mama, who put them back on her nose and said, 'What can you do? That's the way he is.'

They were happy together. She kept him short on money, for she would have had to beg for bread in the streets, in spite of her millions, if she had allowed him to put on the *ferias* that were his daily inspiration. Even Elsie shied away from his dreams of grandeur.

The wife was warm-hearted, short and fat, and no matter who did her hair, or how, it lay on top of her head as if someone had dropped an omelette on it. Her face was round, and the nose, chin, and ears had lost their intended shape and settled into a general mass of rosy dough. She was wrapped in rich, velvety material such as is used for the upholstery of sofas and easy chairs in districts where violent colour is in demand. It can be seen in the windows of furniture stores in Harlem, and in those sections of Los Angeles where Mexicans live.

Mama Korniloff, whose fortune stemmed from San Francisco real estate, loved all that concerned family life, and to celebrate the anniversary of Charles and Elsie she had given Sascha carte blanche.

The parties at the Korniloffs' usually started with a fortified vodka. Ordinary vodka is strong enough. The fortified kind, in which sharp red peppers have been placed, burns your lips and the inside of your mouth, if you're not used to it.

The car was about to start the ascent of the hill atop which the Korniloff mansion stood. It was halted at the bottom, and everybody was asked to get out. There was a tent at the side of the road, and in this the first welcome took place. Korniloff, his eyes already moist, stretched out his arms. Fortunately he greeted Charles first. He clasped him, kissed him, slapped him on the back, then took his hand in both of his and closed his eyes, from which he squeezed two tears to his cheek. I was next, and then came West. We were afraid when it was Elsie's turn. But he stretched out his arms anew and went on his knees. He covered her hands with kisses, and did not squeeze them. Elsie had on the white gloves with the jewels sewn on the outside.

The hot vodka was served, and gypsies played, and the car was dismissed. There is an old Georgian custom of walking to a house and stopping at villages on the way up. Korniloff had built a row of Potemkin villages on the way up to the mansion on the hill.

We made six stops on the way, and at each there were greetings and little hot breads and various other foods, and everywhere the fortified vodka. The host filled the glasses, and everyone drank them down. Charles and Elsie had to empty their glasses at every toast. Eventually vodka, even when fortified, is easy to swallow. The music walked along up the last serpentine, and on top of the stairs, where Sascha usually received, stood his wife, with arms outstretched. She was dressed in the bluest shade in existence, in velour, and she too had tears in her eyes, and she took off the pince-nez the better to be able to kiss everybody heartily. Inside, the big house was so crowded it was like swimming in seaweed. It was hot. The establishment was filled with huge Byzantine bric-a-brac. Madame Korniloff had fallen victim to a decorator who seemed determined to evolve a kind of décor in which all the styles from the Egyptian to Elsie were united and happy under one roof. There were Spanish iron gates inside the house, Louis XIV chairs around a Gothic fireplace, and a Biedermeier porcelain oven at the other end of the same room.

Sascha Korniloff was at home in it. He was in complete rapport with his wife. He said, 'Isn't it peuwtifoowl?' and she smiled her assent.

A trumpet blared, and the signal to eat was given.

The host ploughed through the crowd to a dais in the vast dining-room, on which stood high oak chairs in gilded polychrome around a table covered with cloth of gold. On this table were golden plates, and place cards for the bride and groom and several other guests, as well as the host and hostess. The rest of the guests took places wherever they found them, at tables, on banquettes, and some on the floor.

Our table was as if placed in a tent. The light, as Russians like it, was low; the guitars and cymbals sounded, and the gypsy fiddlers walked about, working wildly at czardas and Cossack melodies, for it was early and not yet the hour for the *chagrin d'amour* melodies.

Mama Korniloff, like Elsie, was a realist. She put an arm shaped like a bowling pin up on the table, put her hand to the side of her mouth, and yelled, 'Elsie!' Then she lifted the cloth of gold to show Mother what was beneath it. The top of this table, recently acquired, was made of the scales of tarpon glued down. Mother inspected it.

Mr Korniloff apologized. 'There is no caviar,' he said. It was impossible to get it just now, and he refused to serve the pressed kind or any other substitute. 'The best or nothing,' he said.

And so there were claws of stone crabs, which are beautiful and heavy as porcelain, followed by all the gourmet dishes of the Russian kitchen—a very fine soup called *tschi*, large salmon baked whole inside a special bread, shashlik brought in on flaming spits, and with it a rough kind of rice flavoured with saffron and with a sauce made of yoghurt.

Elsie, not to discommode anyone's cook at such parties, would go off her Hauser diet and serve herself small portions of what was offered. The host here, however, had seen to the preparation of an extra menu for Elsie. He had ordered a large chicken broiled, and the butler brought a serving table and cut it up with a carving knife. Elsie, who always took the dark meat, leaned towards the host and told him about her childhood and how she had come to like that part of the chicken most. The host again had tears in his eyes as he kissed her.

The gypsies played a few notes of the 'Wedding March' as two men came in and placed a large wedding cake in the centre of the table. On it was written in golden letters, *Elsie and Charles*. Everybody applauded, and the glasses were filled and raised again. Korniloff had detailed one servant to do nothing but keep the glasses at our table filled, and that man was kept busy. The purpose of serving vodka seems to be to light a fire in your insides, which you then try to put out with champagne. Elsie had a big fire going. The butler came again. She had emptied her glass at one draught.

Madame Korniloff put her arm on the table again and called across to Elsie, who turned her head to listen. 'Oh, Elsie,' she screamed, 'Elsie, we're so happy! You know, my oldest daughter is married, and she's been looking for a house—she wants to have the children out here—and just today we found one for sale—a lovely house, it's almost across the street from you.'

Mother let out the seagull cry. 'What?' And then, with the voice of doom, she asked, 'What house are you talking about?'

'You know it, it looks like the one in *Gone with the Wind*.'

Mother said bitterly, 'A very nice house. I hope you get it.'

Madame Korniloff stuck some meat on a fork and nodded, smiling.

Mother said to me under her breath, 'This is a lovely party, but that house isn't going to go with the wind, to anybody except to Mother.' She held up her glass, thinking she could hurry things by making a toast, and she made motions to get up. The butler refilled the glass as Sascha Korniloff got to his feet and knocked on his glass with his fork.

'We must get out of here as quickly as we politely can,' said Mother to me.

Mr Korniloff raised his glass. He had a few words to say. He started to speak with almost closed eyes, and, looking through the slits, he spoke of love and life, marriage, America, ideals, and his friends Charles and Elsie. He sat down to thunderous applause.

A man of the motion-picture industry got up, bowed to Charles and Elsie, and told about his European past, his wife, art for art's sake, his love for America, and money. Then the vodka and champagne seemed suddenly to have done their work. He stopped talking with his mouth open, brought up his right hand, and drew on a violently smoked cigar, half wet from sucking. With his other hand he scratched the back of his neck, then suddenly sat down.

'Any minute now we'll cut the cake,' said the host.

Harry Crocker, who is a brief speechmaker, knocked on a glass and said that Hollywood was a lucky town to have such a nice couple: the happiest couple in Hollywood, and a shining example to all. The glasses were raised, and Charles had to come around and kiss Elsie on both cheeks. The music played, and then Charles got up with glass in hand and said, 'This is not only our wedding anniversary, but also my birthday.'

There was great applause.

'Because on the day I married Elsie I was born anew.'

This brought on thunderous applause and a blast of brass music from a newly arrived orchestra. Mother leaned forward, her elbow on the table, her chin on her fist. At one time Charles had told me that Elsie could curse without opening her mouth. She was cursing now.

Charles continued, 'Our wedding took place at the British Consulate in Paris. We had invited only a few close friends, and when we came we found Mario Panza of the Italian Embassy, and Linda and Cole Porter and Tony Montgomery. The American Ambassador was present, and the British Ambassador, Lord Tyrell, my chief, Duff Cooper and Lady Diana Manners, Lord Inverness and the then Chancellor of the Exchequer. Well, afterwards we sailed from Genoa to Egypt. In the harbour of Alexandria we received an official reception from King Fuad with gun salutes and boat whistles. We stayed there with Sir Nevile Henderson, and we saw Luxor in the moonlight, and suddenly I had some shocking news for my dear wife. I had received news by pouch that, as far as France was concerned, we were not legally married.'

Charles shook with inward laughter, and all the guests joined him.

Elsie had shifted position every second.

'"You're going to get your hat and coat immediately," I said to Elsie, and we went back to France and to the City Hall at Versailles. For in France a marriage is not legal unless it is performed by the mayor of the community in which you reside.'

Charles then started with a new set of names, but ran out of them or else of memory, and he toasted Elsie and finally sat down.

The host got up and announced that Elsie would now cut the cake. There was, however, no proper knife, and one of the butlers ran to the kitchen.

Mother said, 'Where's the knife?' She turned around, and in back of her was the serving table on which her chicken had been carved. The bird was still on it, with only one leg missing. The carving knife lay beside it, the blade submerged in sauce.

Mother kicked her heavy chair around until she could reach the carving knife. The sauce dropped on Sascha Korniloff, who raised both his arms to command silence. Mother got up. She was unsteady and staggered a bit. She sabred through the air and seemed to be fighting a duel with an invisible foe. Finally she located the cake. She let out the seagull cry, 'Ha!' and stuck the knife in, and then pulled it out again to make a second cut.

Charles got up. 'I say, someone take that knife away from Elsie or else call an ambulance—or better, several, for they shall be needed.'

The panic passed. Mother said to me, 'I'm not going to bed tonight. We've got to be there early in the morning.' And, like a child, she said. 'The house! The house! Nobody shall get this house but Mother. As soon as we can we will make our excuses and leave.'

After the cutting of the cake Elsie told Charles that she wanted to leave as quietly as possible, and Charles told the host. He came and said, 'You cannot go, dollink. Rubinstein is comink, Heifetz is comink, Piatigorsky is comink—you will hear music so wonderful as you have never heard in all your life. When I give a party everybody knows it lasts all night, and then in the morning, you know what we do? I have a lake and a houseboat and a few Hawaiians in rowboats playing, and there we will have breakfast and swim. Take a sleep, dear, rest a little, and then come down.'

But Mother shook her head. There was another toast, and then the musicians accompanied us to the door.

'Oh, the car,' said Elsie, 'we sent it back.'

Charles telephoned but nobody answered in the chauffeur's house. Korniloff got his car, a Bentley convertible of which he was very fond, and drove us home.

When we arrived at After All the house was brightly lighted; music was playing. The butler was dancing with Miss Bridget, Susan was waltzing with Achille, and the second man was putting records on the machine while a maid from the Rathbones' stood waiting for him to dance. There were several more couples.

'What's going on here?' asked Elsie.

'Glub, glub, milady, wogs mog mug mag,' said Coombs.

'He's trying to tell you, milady,' Bridget said, 'that we're celebrating milady's and Sir Charles's anniversary.'

'Well, that's very nice,' said Elsie, 'but the next time let us know when you give a party for us, so we can join you.' During these words the room had been restored in lightning fashion, and bottles and ash-trays had disappeared.

Charles had gone to his room. Elsie stood at the end of the corridor and said loudly, 'What do you propose to do about this, Charles?'

Charles came. He was very tired. He said, 'You would never agree, dear. I'd give them all the sack. They thought we'd be out all night. That bounder Coombs opened some of my best wines. Certainly you can't let a thing like this pass without doing something.'

'I know exactly what to do,' Mother said. 'I will charge them rent for the hall and for the drinks and music. You collect it, first thing in the morning, West. Let them pay for it. What's a fair amount?'

West suggested five hundred, but Mother thought that was too much. Make it two.

'That makes it only eight hundred more we need by nine o'clock tomorrow morning.'

Charles closed his door. Mother phoned her attorney in San Francisco and told him to get a plane first thing in the morning, and then she walked to a desk.

'You see, Stevie, this is what drives Mother crazy.'

There was a sign on a green Ming Dynasty statue. It hung around the neck on a green silk cord, and it said, in green ink, 'Do not remove this pencil.'

'Do you see a pencil here, Stevie?'

'No, Mother.'

'That's what I mean, that's what drives Mother crazy. They don't do what they're told. Now, a doctor, or a lawyer, or an artist, or a street cleaner, they have to do their work and they do it; and the President of the United States in Washington does; and everybody else. Only servants think that they don't have to do anything in return for the money they get. Come with Mother. We'll look for a pencil and Mother will make you a rum punch.'

Mother knocked about with glasses and slammed icebox doors. I sat in a kitchen chair. I drank the rum punch slowly.

I remember Mother writing '800' on something, but it may have been in a dream, because it was in immense letters.

The next morning I awoke as usual at eight. I put on a dressing gown and went downstairs. To my surprise, Mother was there with hat and gloves on, ready to go out. She told Coombs to get my breakfast, then said to me, 'Did you sleep well, Stevie?'

'Yes, Mother, I slept very well.'

'Did you know who put you to bed last night?'

'I have no idea.'

'Mother did.'

'Thank you, Mother.'

'And were you comfortable?'

'Yes, very.'

'And warm?'

'Yes, warm.'

'You know why you were warm and comfortable, Stevie?'

'No.'

'Because Mother covered you with her best fur blanket.'

'Thank you, Mother. God bless you.'

'Stevie, do you like that blanket?'

'Yes, I like it very much.'

'Well, Mother will give you that blanket, Stevie.'

I said, 'Thank you very much, Mother.'

She paused. 'Mother will give you that blanket for eight hundred dollars, Stevie.'

14

Mad Dogs and Englishmen

The place at Topango was a cheap tropical paradise. A beach, lost and shifty. Its contours were changed by the wind, the waves, and even the backwash of fishing boats leaving Santa Monica. Nobody wanted to invest money here and build anything. It was a kind of squatters' place where only people possessed of a vagabond nature settled.

My shack was in the shade of the noisiest and most disorderly tree I have ever known. It sounded as if busy squirrels lived in it, but outside of a butterfly or some ants or other mute creatures there was no one, except the tree, to make noises. It twisted with a peculiar sound, a slow, agonized wooden groan, long and intense. It strewed acorns down on the tarpaper roof, and these the wind shifted about like pawns in a game, and eventually some of them were shifted to the edge and fell with a very soft thud into the sand at the front of the shack, or with a harder fall and one or two bounces on the bricked yard in back. It was quiet here. There was only the rhythmic break of the low waves of the Pacific, a sound like *swiiish* in normal time. This changed to the deep boom and crash of water as the wind increased.

Mornings, there was always the impatient parade of seagulls on the roof of the shack.

The sea always provided enough driftwood to keep a fire going, for towards evening it got cool.

Another sound came from the dry leaves that were blown over the brick floor of the courtyard in back of the house. This yard, which was paved by the former owner himself, now was in waves like the sea; there was no level place.

The yard was surrounded by a bamboo fence, six feet high, leading down to the sea and back to an empty space where one could park. Supporting the fence were the trunks of two dead eucalyptus trees and a garage, also built by the owner. Under the living tree was an outdoor shower and outdoor plumbing. It was impossible to go back there without well-soled sneakers, on account of the acorns and the upturned bricks, which hurt your bare feet. Between the bricks grew dandelions and grass.

Inside, the shack was much as it was outside. It had a fireplace of brick, and bamboo furniture. It was one large room divided by partitions into a place with an oven, a large front room, and another next to the kitchen in back, to sleep in. This had an army cot and a mattress. Along the length of the building facing the sea ran a porch, and on this I put my bed, and, having learned from Mother the value of mirrors, I took a large broken mirror from the nails that held it to the wall of the garage, next to the open shower, and attached it diagonally above my bed, so that it reflected the ocean. When I lay in bed I could look up at it, and the white lines of waves breaking on the dark sea, and their sound, put me to sleep.

I came there late at night, after parties, driving by way of Sunset Boulevard, the route that Charles called 'the pretty way'.

I had the top down and the radio going, for it was late and I was tired and had always been drinking, not to drunkenness, but enough—I was used to it and had trained myself to drive carefully, very slowly, and paying attention to every light. A sort of automatic pilot took over. It was not only the sensible thing to do, but also rewarding, for along this route were the night odours of flowers that hang from the trees and plants— lemons in bloom, the night-blooming jasmine, the bittersweet perfume of jusq'aime. Since flowers are always blooming in California, the odours were there every night, along with the voices of the night animals. Then came the view of the sea. There I had to go faster because of the oil trucks, which travelled at about sixty. There was a stretch of about fifteen miles on the highway and then I swung off on a road that was not marked and had no name at the time, and came to the shack. The door of the garage I kept open—I leaned two of the bricks against it when I left in the morning—and I drove in. At that moment the automatic pilot ceased functioning, and every night I touched the end wall of the garage with the bumpers and moved it forward a few inches, so that once a month I had to get the man from the garage in Santa Monica to come with his bulldozer and pull the garage back in place again.

I painted there when the light was good; I sat and watched the sea; and sometimes I drove back to After All the same night; but often I stayed there and slept.

Eventually Sir Charles came, and he was very happy. He undressed in the 'bedroom' and put on shorts, sneakers, and a baby hat, and with his cane he pushed himself along the sand. Beyond my shifty sands, to the right, was a very good proper beach, a stretch that went all the way to the horizon. To the

left there was a water spill down from Topango Canyon, and
past this cold, clear stream, which was about a foot deep, the
beach of Santa Monica began.

On the beach near the house Sir Charles did his exercises,
which he said were very good for him. They were nothing
exceptional or strenuous—mostly the motions he went through
when he had his clothes on. He turned to the right, and then
very importantly to the left, as if looking to see who was on
either side of him at a dinner party. Then he stuck his cane in
the sand and leaned back and held the plum face up to the sky,
and then looked down into the sea. After that he opened and
closed his eyes, and then his hands, making fists and undoing
them again. All this very carefully and mildly. At the end
of these exercises he took his stick and marched up towards
the beach of Santa Monica, with the hope of encountering a
ravishing creature.

The bathing of Charles was as restrained as his exercises.
He floated, he lay in the water, without a wrinkle on his
body from the top of his head to his toes, and he propelled
himself with very small flipperlike motions of the hand; or
else he swam the way people swim after three lessons, very
correctly.

'I can put any man down flat on the ground,' he would say
to a ravishing creature when he found one, and let her feel his
arm. 'It's made of stone.'

'I'm feeling much better. Yesterday I had lunch out somewhere, in a restaurant near the Paramount Studio, very nice.
I prefer Romanoff's, however. At Romanoff's one meets the
awful people one knows. At that other place there are the awful
people one doesn't know.

'I'm eminently improved since I began to come down here. Now, we're having that French wine for lunch, the pink one; don't expect too much of it.'

'Pink wine, Charles, with cold roast beef? Is it done?'

'If I do it, of course it's done... This is the best cure, sand, sun, rest, and sea. The one important thing is, Elsie must never know about this place. She'd find a way of ruining it. I'm fond of her, and I think she's fond of me, but one must have a place to escape to. She's hinted at it, she's heard of it, and only yesterday she said, "I must one day drive down and have a look at Stevie's shack." She added, "You know, he might ask me. I won't be in the way, I'll put a lampshade on my head and sit in a beach chair." I said that there was no beach chair, and then I said that I had a fever of slightly over thirty-seven, which I had, and that I'd have to rest. But she'll try again. Watch out.'

While he was on his beach promenade one day, a patrol car with two officers stopped behind the shack and the policemen came in and said that a mad dog was on the beach, somewhere between Santa Monica and Topango.

The good man John was upset. 'I must go and warn Sir Charles immediately,' he said.

It was almost noon, and illustrated the saying that only mad dogs and Englishmen go out in the midday sun. The officer said to John, 'No, you stay here. We're going towards Santa Monica, and the others have started already from Santa Monica this way.' They walked out and trudged through the sand, looking for the mad dog to shoot.

John always brought along a hamper containing some lunch which Mrs John had prepared—a bottle of milk and some fruit, cold meat, salads, simple things. John set the table in the yard, in the shade of the eucalyptus tree. The table always wobbled; John steadied it and swept up the acorns. While he was busy unpacking lunch Sir Charles walked in.

John said, 'I'm glad to see you, sir, unharmed.'

'Why?'

'There was a mad dog on the beach with you, Sir Charles.'

'Really?' said Charles, and sat down to eat.

One cool, foggy morning he said to me, 'Bemel, one is supposed to know a man seven years before allowing oneself to light his fire. I sat waiting here for you, and it got cold, and I felt that I knew you as well as if it had been seven years. Now, you don't mind, do you?

'I've told you about my fever,' he said. 'These fevers one gets from the various climates out here. There is one climate at the house, another at the Farmers' Market, and a third down here, and then there is the climate of the Valley, and that of the Hills, and since the houses one goes to are located in a variety of climates, one is exposed to danger.

'We're dining out with the assistant French consul tonight, and I daresay one doesn't usually go to an assistant consul's house, but then times have changed. Elsie might need some papers put in order, and he might allow her to send some things by bag—that, dear boy, means by diplomatic pouch.'

These were the usual observations and the routine. Charles left around five.

Slowly the shack became the gathering place for a group of people who liked one another. It was like a little club. Sir Charles was the dean. He managed to get a piano and sang. He smoked cigars. I decorated the inside of the garage, and we put sawdust on the floor. All kinds of people came—actors, singers, writers. We bought beer by the barrel, and sang. We organized extemporaneous theatricals, rehearsed things. The actors played, the singers sang; it was a happy place. It was as if people took vacations from themselves. The stardust was swept away in the brick yard. There was no effort to living—no cleverness in making conversation—no listening to accomplishments and the latest Goldwyn jokes—and even Charles was himself; along with his clothes, he took off the Foreign Office manner.

This repeated itself like the swish of the waves.

15

Kitty Cats and Puthy Cats

N ot long after the anniversary Achille came in
and asked if he could have a word with me. The
Korniloff chauffeur had informed him that Mr
Sascha Korniloff was looking around for somebody to sell his
Bentley to, because he had a chance to get another car even
more glorious than the Bentley convertible.

'Mr Korniloff loves cars the way some people love women,'
said Achille. 'He's absolutely crazy about that Bentley. You've
seen it around—it's the royal-blue job with the black top and
the golden instruments and handles. Because Mr Korniloff
loves that car so much, but cannot afford to keep two sports
cars, he wants to sell one; but he wants to be very sure who
he sells it to.'

So I had been proposed to the Korniloff chauffeur as a
possible candidate, and Sascha Korniloff had investigated me
and found that I might be all right. The price was fair. The car
was in better condition than when new, according to Achille,
and so I became the owner of it.

Mr Korniloff said to me, 'I never let those bastards at hotels
or clubs or night clubs—or, for that matter, anywhere—park

it. No parking attendant touches that car. I hope you continue that. The speed dial is set wrong, so when she goes a hundred miles an hour it shows only eighty, and at seventy, only fifty-five, because I don't want to scare my wife. She can't see the scenery, but she reads the speedometer. She's got aluminium blocks and aluminium pistons'—he was speaking of the car again.

After I gave Korniloff my cheque he said, 'I'm already sorry. If you love a car the way I do you shouldn't sell it. It's like selling a dog you love, you just don't do it.' He fell into a Russian low mood and touched the car and patted the radiator. Achille assured him that the car was in good hands. Korniloff, with moist eyes, looked back at the Bentley twice as he walked away, and Achille was near tears. He took the large flannel and dusted the hood of the car, and then I drove it down to the beach and into the garage behind the shack.

I am car crazy also, and I was very happy. Korniloff, when he had demonstrated it to me, had said, 'This is the best-kept car in the whole wide world. She has a soul and a heart. Listen to her purr along, contented and happy. I know just how much she wants the pressure of my hand, a little more, and now she sings. Look how she takes this curve, look how she goes through traffic! She has a gauge for altitude, a compass that works. This switch is so that when you drive in Paris, you can flash the headlights instead of honking the horn ring. The upholstery is special, and new. I had it made here. The blue carpets are new. There is a cover that goes over the rear compartment when it is not occupied.'

I got a nail in one of the rear tyres, at the beach, and had to have the flat fixed. The car had two spares in the trunk, and

they were both black. The tyres on the car were whitewalls.
So, while the tyre was being fixed, I drove into town with three
white walls, and one black tyre.

Later Korniloff phoned. 'It's raining,' he said.

'I know.'

'Is the car in the garage?'

'Yes.'

'I passed you on the street today. You're not going to drive
around with her that way, I hope.'

'What way?'

'Well, with a whitewall in front and a black tyre in back.'

'I'm picking up the whitewall in an hour.'

He sounded relieved. 'It's like seeing a woman you've loved
appear at a disadvantage, with her hair in disorder or in a bad
dress, when she's with somebody else and you want her to be
as beautiful as she was, so you don't have to be sorry for her.'
He sighed audibly over the phone. 'This new one is a dog.
I'm sorry I got rid of that old darling. This is a super-duper.
The radiator is gold-plated, it has a steering wheel made of
ivory—and it's a whore. I'm a fool for letting the other one
go. Listen, if you ever want to get rid of her, she comes back
to me. With her went a part of my heart. It's awful when I see
her. I can't forget her, and I feel like kicking this one. I forgot,
I have an extra set of things in case you ever take her hunt-
ing—watertight covers for the seats and extra carpets for the
floor. I'll bring them over.

'Forty-one was a very good year for cars. You know, I washed
her myself. It was like giving a new mistress a bath, all over.
I washed her and then took a chair and sat in the garage and
just looked at her. And am I jealous now, when I see you in

that car, that like a fool I sold her.' He said goodbye with deep Russian sadness and hung up very softly.

Mother said, 'It's perfectly wonderful, that car, and I'm so glad for you. Let Mother have a ride in it. Just drive Mother around the block.'

Korniloff came to the garage and watched Achille wash the car and supervised the work and polished the car and adjusted the motor and also the rearview mirrors. 'I am a fool, a goddam fool. I know I will not be happy with the new one. That whore on wheels!'

Driving down to the beach one day, I passed him. He was in his new car and made such a disgusted face that his nose almost touched his chin. I stopped, and he stopped. 'Listen,' he said and raced the motor. 'Awful, no? Look at this instrument panel! It's like a boudoir, bedroom clocks in a row; and this ivory steering wheel, it has a bad feeling. I must have been drunk when I got her. Do you drive down to the beach a good deal? Well, then, you better have her waxed so the sea air will not corrode her.

'A car can do all the things for you a woman can, and also do all the things to you a woman can. It can kill you, it can make you happy, leave you flat; you can get mad at it, leave it for another one, and then find out too late that the old one was the one you really cared for. Well, as I said, if you ever want to get rid of her I'll be there. I'll give you back what you paid for her.'

On days of fog and storm I stayed at the house in town. Achille always brought the car to the door in the morning, and I drove to the studio. One day, as he gave it a last rub with the flannel, he looked shocked.

'It's those damn kitty cats and puthy cats of Miss West that does that,' he said, pointing to scratches on the hood of the car. 'It gets cold toward evening, and the cats like this car because the hood is almost flat and she's warm when she gets in, so they lie there. We gotta do something about that.'

Coombs came out of the house and looked at the hood disapprovingly, and Achille told him about the cats.

For several days I drove to the studio with the hood of the car marred by cat scratches. Achille was worried; he said, 'We'd better get it fixed before Mr Korniloff sees it.'

'But how about the cats? They'll scratch it up again.'

'Them kitty cats and puthy cats, they won't bother that car no more, sir, after today. Coombs saw to that.'

Achille came close and informed me that Coombs had made a mixture of red pepper, black pepper, and Sir Charles's snuff, and put this on the hood of the car for three nights, in liberal doses, and the cats had not been near the car since; so it was safe to get it polished and have the scratches removed.

The polishing was to be done the next day, and at the same time the car would be waxed. That evening Mother wanted to go to a restaurant half-way between Los Angeles and Santa Monica, a place recently opened and highly recommended. At the table next to us was Mr Halvah, with an actor who played tough guys and gangsters. They both looked unhappy. Mr Halvah, whose greeting was usually very polite, ignored Mother. He looked away. He seemed absent.

A character waiter, old and thin, handed us an immense menu. Mother studied it and the dialogue at the next table, which went like this:

Halvah: 'I'm fine.'

'Yeah?'

'Sure I'm fine.'

'Don't care, eh?'

'No, I'm through.'

'Ah, is that so?'

'I read the paper, see. I like to read the paper in bed, you know, when I come home. I like to get into bed and read. That was the trouble. She suddenly screams, "Turn out the light and go to sleep."'

'Oh yeah, as simple as that? I bet you don't read the paper now.'

'This time it's going to cost me plenty.'

'Yeah, they don't like guys to beat up their wives in this town.'

Mr Halvah pulled up his trouser leg and showed the marks of a deep bite on his leg.

'Oh, that's going to be fine. You're going to show that in court?'

'No, the doctor will testify. I have a very good doctor—'

'Never hit a woman. Most of the time you hit the radiator anyway.'

'It was self-defence.'

'You haven't got a chance. Imagine a bully like you striking a woman! They'd let her go if she shot you.'

'So I pay.'

'Yes, you pay. How does it feel, kind of lonesome?'

Mr Halvah shrugged his shoulders.

'When you think of her, that don't feel so good, does it? Maybe she's not alone, maybe there's a guy with her now.'

Mr Halvah shrugged his shoulders again.

The other put on a malicious smile, with the wings of the nose pulled back, and said, 'Maybe there's a guy going through that golden hair with his fingers and breathing on her now.'

'Listen, you so-and-so sonofabitch!' cried the tortured Halvah and almost knocked over the table as he left.

Mother said to me, 'I'm very seldom wrong in my judgement of people. Mr Halvah seemed such a nice man... Look over there, Stevie, there is the gallant Sir Charles Mendl escorting a ravishing creature to a table.'

The interior of the restaurant was like an oriental tent. In the centre a fountain played. The head waiter wore a dinner jacket and white shoes, and there was a hostess named Queenie. One of the specialities of the place was Ham Steak en Plank. The name on the china was that of some other restaurant, the prices were very steep, and the silver seemed to have come from a five-and-ten-cent store.

The maître d'hôtel approached. He spoke French as if Mischa Auer had taught him, and he recommended another speciality of the house, crêpes Suzettes.

'Zee sugaire for ziss crêpes Zusette, Madame and Monsoor, she is kept in jar, to age from five to ten years togezzer with vanilla beans—iss like everything we zerve here, in ziss faine restaurant—iss like pearls and diamonds.' This last statement was an illusion to which the proprietor and the cashier also subscribed.

The crêpes Suzettes were good. Elsie went off her Hauser diet. It was a nice place to sit and watch people, but then a man at the table to the left ordered a cigar, and the head waiter in the white shoes brought it, carefully, on an imitation silver tray. It was a ten-cent cigar with the band that identified it removed.

The maître d'hôtel held it to his ear. Rolling it between his fingers, he smelled it, then cut off the end. He said, 'Ziss is zee real hand-made Cuban zigaar, made zpecial for ziss restaurant.'

Mother collected her belongings, and I asked for the bill. She said, 'It's a lovely evening. You know, Stevie, it would make Mother happy if you'd show Mother that little place on the beach, now that we're so close to it.'

'I don't think you'd like it, Mother. It smells of cigars, the linen hasn't been changed for a month, and it has no plumbing. It's not the kind of a place that you would like at all.'

'Unless you or Charles has installed some ravishing creature there, who you are ashamed to let the world know about, Mother wants to see the shack.'

'Very well, then, I'll show it to you.'

It was nine-thirty and a little windy, and we were almost at the sea and driving through the main street of Santa Monica at thirty-five miles an hour when Mother said, 'I wonder if you'd put up the top. I love the open air, but this is a little too much.'

I put up the top, and there was a draught from the open side windows, so I closed them. To get some air into the car I pulled the lever that opens the ventilator, which is located in front of the windshield on the hood of the car. At once I was in terrible pain, and blind. Some of the mixture of red pepper, black pepper, and snuff had blown in my eyes and choked me. I lost my sense of direction. I saw something glowing red coming at me and tried to avoid it. I turned the wheel. The car jumped. There was a crash of glass.

Mother coughed. She had got some of the stuff also. Luckily she was dozing, and it had not got into her eyes. Vision came back to me, and I saw a curious assortment of things in the windshield: about a dozen small photos of Clark Gable in plastic frames, tea cups, baskets, percolators, teddy bears, a kids' chemical set, artificial roses, blue and red composition books, and the price tags of all these things. Slowly it became clear to me that we were sitting inside the window of a drugstore in Santa Monica. Then I saw that it would be fatal to move, for we sat as if under the knife of a guillotine. Pieces of the broken pane were above us.

'I hope you're insured,' said Elsie in the tone in which she usually spoke to Charles.

'Yes, I'm insured.'

'And luckily you're not drunk.'

'Yes, luckily.'

The police siren whined, and a patrol car came, and the policemen got us out.

'Your licence, please.'

'You the writer?'

'Yes, I am.'

'I'm a member of the Book-of-the-Month Club.'

'Now, isn't that wonderful?' said Mother.

'You been drinking?'

'No.'

'You better sit down in the police car anyway. If people see you swaying they'll think you're drunk.'

The cop told his partner to stay with the Bentley, and he reported the accident by telephone from his car and directed that a wrecking car should be sent to tow it away.

'I'll take you home, lady,' said the cop. 'What's the address?'

I gave him the address in Beverly Hills, but Mother said, 'Can you get on that phone and call my house, and have my chauffeur Achille come and pick me up? We're going to a little shack on the beach. Mr B. here will give you the address.'

The officer telephoned and then drove on with us as passengers.

Mother said, 'Is there anything, officer, that I can do for you? Is there a favour I can do for you, or your wife, or your children—anything—does your wife need an operation, do you want to send your son to college—anything—would you like a case of whisky?'

The officer shook his head. 'Nope,' he said. He was happy, he wasn't married, he had no children, and he didn't smoke or drink.

We came to the shack, and I made a fire out of old coat hangers. Elsie inspected the place and shook her head. The officer said, 'There is something *you* can do for me, Mr B. I told you I was a member of the Book-of-the-Month Club. Well, I'm also a writer. I have written a story, a scenario, and it's outside in the car. May I bring it in?'

He brought it. It was as thick as a New York telephone directory. He carried it under his arm. In the other hand he carried an emergency lamp with a huge battery, and he sat down and began to read: 'Virginia di Milo, who traded the love and security of a good home to become a glamour actress in Hollywood, was that poor girl, Gertrude Smith from Brooklyn, found dead of malnutrition in a cheap room in Santa Monica. The scene opens in the home of a broken-hearted mother…'

Mother tiptoed out, waving goodbye to me in back of the policeman. I heard Achille talking to her outside, and then the door slammed and the car slowly drove off.

16

Late for Dinner

For other people disaster comes in threes. For me it seems to come in fours. Disaster number one was not running into the drugstore window but the scenario of Officer Craig. He returned the next day with madman's eyes and asked almost at the point of the gun if this was not the Greatest Scenario Ever Written, and it was not. Being taken from life, it was so wild and improbable that no one would have had the courage to produce it. I took my life in hand and told him so. I said that in gratitude for his great kindness I would see if M-G-M would make a movie of the script, that is, if he would allow me or them to make certain changes. At this he bristled and said not a line would be changed. The climate at the beach became infected with visits by the patrol car, and, all in all, it would have been easier, and I would have seen less of the police, if I had been drunk the night of the accident, and been arrested, and been sentenced to the six months in jail that drunken driving gets you in California. I told that to Officer Craig, and he was very hurt.

He continued his visits, however, and this led to disaster number two, in a chain reaction involving four disasters in a period of two months.

Around that time Mother looked at me and said, 'You're getting fat, Stevie, and it's not good for you. Stop eating and drinking the way you do, and go on Hauser's diet, and take some exercise. Now, even Charles takes exercise regularly. Why don't you?'

I hate exercise, with the one exception of riding. I would not have done that except for Officer Craig, who arrived at the shack between four and five every day when he returned from his routine patrol. I thought that would be a good time to get some exercise. There was a wonderful woman, truly a ravishing creature, Liz Whitney, living on a ranch on the way to Topango, and she had horses, and she had told me any time I wanted to ride, just to go out and ask for a horse.

So I took Mother's advice, followed the Hauser diet, and also went out to Liz's—and into disaster number two. There was a horse, also a ravishing creature, a black mare that no one could ride. Her previous owner had had her at the race course, and she had torn down the starting machinery, bucked off the jockey, and raced by herself ahead of the field. She was too good to shoot, and he had given the mare to Liz. In the stables there was a second black mare. The horses were as alike as twins, with the one difference that the one was docile and sweet and the other mad. The plot was completed by the presence of a new groom at the hour of my arrival, and the absence of Liz. For she had told me to 'ask for the black mare'. So the groom saddled the black mare, naturally the wrong one, and I rode up into the mountains.

There is a road, macadam part of the way, that leads back into Coldwater Canyon and then goes sharply uphill in a narrow rising path which is bordered, or was then, by tight growth, big trees and small. This is like a green tunnel, and eventually, at the timberline, it gives way to rocky scenery, boulders left and right. To the left of the boulders immense bulldozers had changed the landscape. They stood in the far distance, looking like immense yellow insects intent on quick devouring. They had smoothed enough terrain to build a village on, torn the brush and trees from it. The upturned earth was burnt sienna in colour, and soft.

The mare was very good on the macadam, and in the greenery she looked left and right, as interested horses do. She was beautiful in motion, she danced, and when she came out of the greenery she went upwards as I have never been carried, light as a ballet dancer, elegant and fast; her nostrils quivered, and she chose the path surefootedly. It was the greatest ride I have ever been on, and a rare pleasure. I like the high places.

We were almost to the top of the mountain. There was nothing much ahead, perhaps another two hundred feet of climbing. Below was the great panorama of green and blue, the ocean and the city, and ahead of me was a firebreak, a wide strip of earth shorn through scrub oak and brush. It's like the strip of scalp a tribe of Indians shave across the top of their heads, and here its purpose is to stop fires from advancing from one mountainside to the other. A fresh wind blew up here, and it looked like a racetrack, and here the mare decided to go, and she ran with the speed of the wind. I realized then that it would be tough.

I thought, Let her go, she'll exhaust herself, just try and stay on. I stayed on for a run to the end of the track and back. I was cold; I was wearing only a shirt and jodhpurs, and no hat. It would have been all right, for she didn't try to buck me off. It would have been fine if she had become exhausted. But after the return trip she decided to go home at the speed she had been going. She was a most intelligent horse. I kept talking to her, trying to make her listen to reason. I said all the sweet things I could think of, and she had her ears back a good deal of the time.

She found the path back home, and now we were on a dive down the mountain. She had lost weight and sweated, the saddle girth was loose, and I knew I had to get off, but I wanted to choose where to do it. I looked for a good place to fall, and I remembered Charles's advice about polo falls. One always makes the mistake of looking for a soft place, a bed of mosses preferably, and that is altogether fatal. The forest was ahead. In sudden caprice she might brush me off on a tree trunk or low branch, so there were only a few seconds in which to decide where to fall, and I said to myself, Now, in a second or two. She went well in spite of the fast descent, and perhaps, after all, the thing was to trust her and to ride on and take a chance on the trees. We were down to where the bulldozers had softened the ground, and I thought that the best bet would be to get the mare on that ground, for the soft earth would hold her back and tire her quickly, and then she could be ridden home.

I tried to collect her to turn her towards that terrain, but the moment she felt the reins she stood up, snorted, and jumped over a boulder. I thought she'd break my neck and hers. She raced down the path. Now the decision had to be made, there was no more choice, and just as I started to count, *one, two, three,* the animal fell and rolled over, and I hit something with my head, and, as people always say in such circumstances, everything suddenly went black. When I woke up it was dark, and after I realized where I was I got up. Nothing was broken. I was merely freezing. And then I saw the outline of the crazy mare. She was grazing nearby.

I went and talked to her softly, and I was very glad she stayed, for there is nothing sillier than a rider walking back after he has fallen off his horse. She was very friendly. She kept on cropping the small plants off the ground as if nothing had happened, and then she raised her head while chewing. She looked at me with very intelligent eyes. She let me take the reins, and I led her back to the road. At first I thought I'd lead her to a place where she'd be blocked in by rocks and get on her, but then I felt it wasn't necessary. Animals have souls and greater sensitivity than people. They must have, for they live by their senses alone, and nobody has told them anything about life; nor can they read or inform themselves except by experience and intuition. I had a great moment of animal communion and friendship there on the mountain. She nudged me and almost pushed me up into the saddle. She went down, all gentleness, as if carrying an invalid, and in fact she was. I had been unconscious for about four hours. Liz had come back and sent out people to look for me when she found that the crazy mare had been saddled. Nobody thought of the mountain, and in this region, where a lot of riding is done, there are tracks everywhere, and it's hard to find anybody.

As I went into the living-room of the ranch house I discovered in the mirror that I was smeared with blood. I had been bleeding from nose and mouth. I washed and then drove home.

I changed and came down, and Mother said severely, and again in the tone she used to Charles, 'Stevie, you're late for dinner.'

Stories of violence and adventure bored Mother, and so I said nothing of what had happened. I had a desire to yawn all during dinner. Korniloff came. He had been to supervise the repairs on the Bentley. After dinner I shook, and felt sick and went to bed, and the next day I was taken to the Cedars of Lebanon, with virus pneumonia. But that was not the final disaster either, for there was penicillin, and an oxygen tent, typically Hollywood, with a telephone in it, and the good Dr Schliff. In a room above Hedy was having another baby, and the nurse who combed Hedy's hair took the black strands that she combed out and rolled them up and put them on the window sill, and a bird came and carried them off to make a nest of them with other less romantic materials in a nearby tree.

Disaster number three happened while I was a patient.

I had visits every day. Charles gave me no warning of what was happening on the outside, and neither did Mother, except that she told me she would have a big surprise for me when I got out of the hospital.

When I was cured Mother sent Achille with her car to take me to the beach, for the surprise.

Suddenly I stood in front of what had been my shack, and it was now an extension of After All. There was a pavilion where the rickety table had stood. The inside of the house was the latest in modern beach living. It was well thought out and sensible, and even beautiful. One wall of the bedroom was an immense mirror; the closet space, so important to Elsie, was perfect; the lighting fixtures were of material stretched over metal frames; the carpeting, woven raffia squares in sand colour. The terrace had been widened, and it had a deck with beach chairs and umbrellas, and a playhouse with veranda and dressing room at the edge of the water. There were plants and flowers everywhere. My picture that I was so happy about, the one with the old ragged bamboo screen hanging half-way down the window and the rusty can with the marguerite in it, was framed, and it hung there like a bleeding heart. It was the only reminder of the old days.

Mother was enchanted, and she took me around, holding me by the arm, and showed me the various gadgets: the working desk, the buttons for the light, the bathroom, the heater, and the refrigerator. The wind still shook the whole house, for she had left the frame as it was. There was a green telephone. Mother was happy.

'Now you've got a place to live in,' she said, and then she sat down on the couch and poked me in the ribs. 'And you know, Stevie, it won't cost you a cent, not a single red penny.'

'How is that, Mother?'

'Well, you know the money you contributed to Tara? Well, this is done with the profit on that, twenty-two thousand, and Mother will give you back your original investment because Mother loves you.'

I have never had greater difficulty thanking anybody.

But that again, in this chain of events, was not the ultimate disaster. The next blow followed one day later.

Charles came to the beach and in German said, '*Die alte Frau*, after ruining our peaceful hideaway down here, is about to do you another favour. In fact, it's done already—she has found the perfect servant for you. He's engaged and starting tomorrow.'

At the house Mother sat close to me and poked me in the ribs again. 'Stevie, Mother has found the perfect servant for you. He has the most wonderful aura, and the most wonderful recommendations. Now, tomorrow Mother will come to the beach and establish a routine for him. He's a Frenchman who's been in America some time—very presentable. He can drive, valet, cook. His demands are modest, and he's so good that I wouldn't mind having him myself instead of that awful blub-goob Coombs. This one you can understand. He speaks like an actor. I have told him about your house, and he is delighted to work in a bohemian household. Now, that is settled, and Mother can stop worrying about you. The man's name is Pierre. He's reporting at nine tomorrow morning, ready for work, and you won't live like a gypsy in a wagon any more.'

Pierre was all that Mother had promised. Sober, decent, understanding. He washed the car and pressed clothes, and he was a friend rather than a servant. He was an excellent cook and knew wines, and he was well read and liked pictures. He did too much work, never asked for a day off. He liked being around the house, and he was always busy fixing something.

I don't have any feeling about a thousand people working for somebody else. It's like a hotel, and I don't mind people who work in a place that is a restaurant or hotel, but I am uncomfortable having someone work for me solely, who is around me all the time. Pierre was on call twenty-four hours a day, mostly audibly near, shining something or where I could see him.

He enquired about the temperature desired in the bath, in the living-room, in the bedroom. He sensed all my dislikes and preferences. He seemed to be psychic also, because when I came to the beach house at an unusual hour of the night the fire was burning, whisky and soda were ready, a sandwich in the icebox. The only thing wrong was that while he was there

I couldn't do a stroke of work. The picture with the rusty can did not altogether satisfy me yet. I wanted some fishing boats in it. I had placed them mentally. I got my paints and put three boats into the picture, and that was suddenly the bad part of it, and I was unhappy about them.

Mother was certainly psychic, for she sensed that I wasn't happy, and she didn't talk about it or come visiting.

She said only once, when I was thinking about the beach house, 'Stevie, you know you can sublet it for a good price. Mother will do it for you if you want her to.'

The films I was working on were almost finished. My contract had only a month to go, and I had taken a job with a magazine to go to Europe and do a series of articles for them.

Charles came and said that the coloured butler of the Munchins had given notice because he wanted to return to Paris. I told Pierre that it would be a good opportunity for him, and Charles recommended him to Munchin, and he left.

He was back on his first day off and asked if I minded if he straightened out the house. He missed the beach. He said Mr Munchin, his new employer, washed his own socks and went about the house picking up little pieces of soap and sticking them on big pieces. He leaned a chair against his bedroom door at night to brace it, besides locking it. On all the windows were locks, and the liquor was locked up. There was an accounting system for everything. The eggs and all other items were doled out, and the servants went into town to eat at their own expense, for the food at the house was insufficient and nothing to look forward to—baked beans and hot dogs, spaghetti and meatballs, things like that. 'Strange how some people live, with all the money in the world. Now with all he's got, to be like that. The only money they spend is on parties, because Madame wants to get into society.

'When there's a party there's plenty of everything, and after the guests leave he locks up the liquor again, and he turns himself into a garbage can, eating what's left over, and what he can't eat is locked up also, and served the next few days. We had leftover cocktail sandwiches for lunch the other day. I'm staying because he asked me to go with them to Paris, all expenses paid—that is, I'll get a cabin in tourist. He asked me for a list of the best places in Paris, restaurants, night clubs, hotels, and so on. He already had several lists, and he checked one against the other, and then, you know what he did?

'He had dozens of pictures of himself, passport pictures, made, and he pasted these on the back of postal cards. The front of the postal card showed a housing development called Munchintown, and then he had typed under his photographs: "There's more to come. I'm Julius A. Munchin, arriving on the *Queen Mary* on such and such a date, and staying at the Hotel Georges Cinq." He attached a five-dollar bill to each of the cards and put them into envelopes, which he addressed to the people who run these places. How impressed they will be!'

The last week at the studio there arrived by air a large wooden box with many markings on it: to keep it cold, to open carefully. And I found that it contained a ten-pound can of caviar in dry ice: the best, the largest, the grey-green beads, the first that had been shipped in a long time. It was sent to me as a gift by Ernie Byfield, the owner of the Ambassador Hotel in Chicago.

Charles and I had planned a farewell party at the beach for the friends of the old days, and the caviar came in handy.

The problem was where to keep it until the party took place. The icebox at the beach was too small. Mrs John's icebox was crammed. There was only the huge refrigerator at home. So I had the caviar wrapped in a very serious fashion, put it in a square box, and wrote a label for it. Since I had just come out of the hospital I wrote, 'Sulfa and penicillin, for emergency use'; under that, my name, and then I tied it up and sealed it with sealing wax, and at the house I handed it to Susan to be kept in the refrigerator in a dry compartment.

'Very clever the way you arranged that, dear boy,' said Charles.

It was the evening hour again, and Mother descended the stairs, and took my arm, and wandered about looking at the menageries and the pictures, and then she took her stance and suddenly said, 'Stevie, you have a box in our refrigerator.'

'Yes, Mother.'

'What's in it?'

'You know I just came out of the hospital, Mother, and it's sulfa and penicillin for emergency use.'

'It's not the kind of black penicillin we put on crackers for cocktails, Stevie, is it?'

This was so unexpected I had no answer ready.

'Stevie, you're not going to give a party down at that lovely beach house that Mother made for you without inviting Mother? What, ha?'

I had had time to catch up. 'I wanted it to be a surprise party for Mother.'

Mother danced and knocked about on one leg and kicked with the other, and she made all her faces of joy. 'Stevie, we're driving down to the beach tomorrow, and Mother will take care of all the details. A beach party! I've always wanted to have a party at the beach! We'll have the most wonderful beach party there ever was!'

Later I went to inspect the box out in the refrigerator. It had not been tampered with. The cord and seal and the label, all were intact. Mother was indeed psychic.

17

The Visit to San Simeon

At the anniversary party Harry Crocker had given me an invitation on behalf of Mr Hearst to visit San Simeon. I told Mother that I had accepted, and was very interested to see the man and the establishment.

'You will have a wonderful time, Stevie. Mr Hearst is devoted to things that are beautiful. He has an immense collection of everything. I only wish I could come along.'

I drove off, and some three hundred and forty miles from Los Angeles I turned off the highway, to the right, at a sign that read 'San Simeon'.

I came to a cottage where a gatekeeper checked my invitation—he was in dungarees and a cowboy hat. He took hold of a rope and pulled on it, and a gate of a peculiar construction, an immense gallows, swung up and over the car. I drove on, and the gate swung back down. I continued on, and a mile past the private airport I came to another gate. This was unattended and of different construction from the first. A long metal rod lay on the ground. At the end of it was a cradle on to which the left front wheel of the car is driven. This puts in motion a mechanism that swings the gate open.

I passed over an identical cradle at the exit from the gate, which shut it behind me. On this side of the gate, under a sign giving instructions for its use, was another sign warning visitors not to leave their automobiles on account of the presence of wild animals.

I passed two more of these gates as I drove towards San Simeon. I was now about a thousand feet above sea level, and on the hills, in the valleys, and on patches of sunlit grass appeared the wild animals.

There were wandering herds of zebra, of yaks, of water buffalo, springbok, and deer of every description in a landscape that must be as big as a country. The animals were used to cars, and as I went on, the heads of a dozen bison appeared a few feet from the windscreen. It is strangely simple, like turning the pages of a children's book. 'Look, look! A zebra. Look, a yak! Papa Buffalo, Baby Buffalo. See the horns on the gazelle—the stripes on the zebra!' This simplicity is part of the whole establishment and comes at you again and again.

At a turn in the road I found myself close to the top of the hill, and there stood the castle. It was best described by a child who was brought here late at night for a visit and saw the castle for the first time lit up. The child softly began to sing 'Happy birthday to you'.

It is a mixture of a cathedral and a Spanish hilltop city with a piece of California suburb placed at its feet. It has the feeling of a community built by a monastic order that says mass with castanets. It is extremely Catholic in feeling, like Mont St Michel, but with a fat top to it instead of a sharp pencil-shaped church steeple. It has all the characteristics of monuments built by man to the glory of himself and God.

The car stops where Nature ends and the monument begins. You have the same tourist-like feeling as at the base of the pyramid of Gizeh, or at the entrance to the Taj Mahal.

The gatekeeper below had announced the approach of the car, and down from the castle came a plain, friendly woman such as might run a middle-class hotel. She is the housekeeper, and she assigns living quarters to the arriving guests. She said, 'I'll send somebody for the bags.' I climbed four terraces and entered a vast hall panelled with the ancient choir stalls of a Gothic cathedral.

One of the dark walnut choir stalls functions as a door. The seat has been removed. I passed through this and came out in a cement vault, cold, dark, and draughty. In this stands an octagonal cement tube that holds an elevator. The elevator is self-operating and has room for three people. The inside of the elevator is again disguised with the worm-holed wood of old church furniture—perhaps the panelling of several confessionals. In this I rode up to the top, to the tower apartment assigned to me, which is called the Celestial North. It is composed of a bathroom on the first landing, and above this, via a winding stairway, a living-room, and over this a bedroom. This is in the very top of the tower. The bedroom is octagonal and about twenty feet in diameter, with a heavy inlaid gold ceiling—as are all the ceilings here. Between the massive beams are recessed spaces decorated with the things one finds on tapestries and carpets: jewel-coloured fragments of flowers and fishes, birds and heraldry. Some of these are the work of original artists of hundreds of years ago. But frequently, as in this apartment, they are supplemented by 'antiqued' new painting. There is no undecorated space: doorposts, hinges, niches, balconies, and the accessories to them, the things that support them, are all decorated. The only vacant and airy spaces—and they come upon you suddenly as you open a door—are unfinished corridors, lofts, stairs, and passages where the cement seems still to be wet and bears the grain of the wood mould in which it was poured. Sticking out everywhere are the iron staves, like walking sticks, that you see in unfinished concrete construction work.

The furniture in the bedroom of the Celestial North consisted of a bed and two cabinets. The bed stood in the centre, a four-poster of tremendous weight, and again carved and painted. On the wall were curtains twenty feet in length, gold brocade, with draw cords so that you could pull all of them closed and find yourself in an octagonal tent of gold. The two old glass cabinets were to the left and right of the bed. But there was no place to hang your clothes, so I hung mine on the wire coat hangers that a former tenant had left hanging on the arms of two six-armed gold candelabra, five feet high, on either side of the bed. On these I hung almost everything; the rest I put on the floor. There was no chair, no closet.

The bathroom below was done with mirrors and golden fixtures, and while there would have been plenty of room for a bathtub, there was none—but again, a museum piece of woodcarving, another cabinet, and a shower stall. In this apartment the water was connected up wrong, so that hot water came out of both taps. I never thought cold water important in the bath, as long as you have enough hot water. The cold you take for granted. In a tub you can let hot water cool, but not in a shower. With hot water from both taps you are defeated.

I thought of calling up, but then I found there was no phone. So I only shaved; and, after soaking a towel in hot water, I let it cool and bathed in the wet towel.

You are all alone up here. You can scream as loud as you wish and make any other noises you please; nobody will hear you. You try to look out at the magnificent scenery, but there is golden stuff at the windows. They are dusty, blind with a historic patina. And outside the windows is heavy golden scrollwork. Besides, on each window there hangs a sign, printed by hand on a piece of cardboard like the ones in shirts from the laundry, that says: 'Please do not open the window.' These signs, tied to the handles of the windows with string, are on all four windows of the eight walls.

On the inside of the elaborately carved door hangs a carbon copy, on half a sheet of typewriter paper stuck there with a tack, of the hours at which meals are served:

> Breakfast—10:30 to 11:30
> Luncheon—1:30
> Dinner—8:30

It was around six when I left the Celestial North suite and tried to find my way back, first passing through the cement vault, then into the octagonal confessional that is the elevator, then through the dark cement vault below, coming out eventually through the choir stall, and finding myself in the living-room. This is half of Grand Central Station. The stalls go up to a height of twenty feet. Above them hang tapestries—for two of which Michelangelo did the sketches, and four others of heroic dimensions. Phoebe Apperson Hearst paid two million dollars for those four alone. In the four corners of the room stand statues—marble women of the anonymous type of nude holding a piece of drapery to her lower abdomen, leaning forwards, the arms pleasantly arranged. Three of them are just statues. In the fourth corner is a special one—a very fine Grecian woman, with eyes such as are set into stuffed animals, that came from some London palace and cost a hundred and twenty thousand dollars.

Looking with the eyes of Elsie, I wondered about her genie, Good Taste, and the three attendants, Simplicity, Suitability, and Proportion. Couches all over, and in one corner, hiding the lower half of the marble woman, a radio cabinet done to match the room—a bad Gothic imitation of such woodcutting as the Riemenschneider altars in Southern Bavaria, with figures in a very foreshortened perspective, and characters too lachrymose or too much in motion and out of control, and with dark stuff smeared into the deep parts to make it antique.

In the centre of the room was a fireplace that reached the sixty-foot ceiling, and this by contrast was superbly beautiful—perhaps the rarest fireplace in the world—of great tenderness, magnificent colour, a breathless living monument, a perfect thing, big as the façade of a house.

A few feet away stood a dreadful rosewood piano with a carmine coverlet of the unhappiest texture and shade.

Next to the awful things and the beautiful things were the sad. There were two long boxes, polished old-fashioned ste-reopticons. I sat down on a high chair and twisted two black handles, adjusting the lenses to my eyes, and the machine lit up and showed a series of slides. As I turned there appeared scenes of travel—Mr Hearst in Venice, in Bad Nauheim, in

Nuremberg, in Switzerland, on a road in the Dolomites, and
leaning on a fountain in a street in Rothenburg; sometimes
alone, sometimes in a group, but in every picture he was like
a stranger, not the person who was photographed, but somebody cut from another picture, always the same, and pasted
into the setting.

I walked through the dining hall. It is formidably Gothic.
Up above hang the old, torn battle flags of the city of Siena.
Below is a table the length of the room, so big that whoever
sits at the far end is very small. Here again is a fireplace that
devours the trunks of trees. The flames, behind a glass screen,
leap up to the height of a man. At the right is an armourer's
anvil, arresting and beautiful, but the base of it is fixed to hold
nuts, and on top of the anvil lies a hammer to crack the nuts.
There are tall silver altar candlesticks all along the centre of
the long refectory table, and between them stand, in a straight
line and in repeating pattern, bottles of catsup, chilli sauce,
pickled peaches, A.1. sauce, salt and pepper in shakers that
are cute little five-and-ten-cent figures of Donald Duck with
silvered porcelain feet, and glasses in which are stuck a handful
of paper napkins.

The kitchen is immense. The large oven is operated by a
blowtorch-like device that spouts oil. The smaller ovens work
by electricity. (The entire castle is electrically heated—the bill
is twenty-five hundred dollars a month.)

On a blackboard in the pantry I saw several notices tacked
up—all written and signed by Mr Hearst. One said: 'Keep the
meals simple. No meat for breakfast, except bacon; and for
lunch, use stews; for dinner only meat. The guests must be on
time for meals. No trays in rooms. Try and keep the food for

the staff as much like that of the guests as possible. Simplify and cut down whatever you can.'

The kitchen was clean. The butler was a German, a small thin man. His wife, a curious creature, looked the way she should in this house—like a polychrome figure, also of the Nuremberg-altar period, with a round nest of golden hair; and she had that face which they must then have thought pretty. By our sense of design today, she had the look of a gargoylish cellar-and-moat beast with blinking eyes and a birdlike, hopping walk, just right among the choir stalls.

I wandered into a billiard room with the most beautiful tapestry of the lot, and then down to the kennels.

I had noticed a sign at one of the automatic gates: 'Dogs not allowed, except in kennel.' In these kennels, in long rows of runways, were about two hundred dachshunds of every shape and size and dachshund kind—black, brown, long-haired, short-haired, crossbred with soft long-haired. They all were yapping and running. As I looked at these dogs, which were born in these kennels and live and die in them, a visitor to the castle, who was about to leave and was making his last tour, joined me. The way one would leave a farmer friend's with a box of eggs, and debate whether it was worth the trouble, this departing guest looked at the dogs and said, 'I wonder should I take along a dachshund?' But, a true lover of dogs, he answered himself, 'No, I'm out too much. I don't want to make a dog lonesome.'

I went back to the living-room and found a group of people—all business faces, executives. They were talking about 'the Chief', exchanging polite stories that made him human, great, but with weaknesses that a great man could afford.

I had often heard that liquor at the castle was taboo. But the butler came in with a large silver tray and set up everything anybody wanted to drink.

While he mixed martinis there was a call from the far end of the room for one of the executives. He shouted across the room, 'Find out who it is.' The man who had the phone shouted back, 'It's Archie.' 'Archie who?' asked the executive. 'Archbishop Spellman,' said the man at the phone. 'Well, all right,' said the executive, 'I'll take it in the other room.'

Presently the huge glass and iron door, on which hung another laundry-cardboard sign, saying, 'Keep this door closed', opened. Two dachshunds that had escaped the fate of the others in the kennels below flitted across the floor and jumped on one of the couches, and Mr Hearst came into the room.

I have often observed that men who have to do with property walk with one shoulder held higher than the other. That is the way Mr Hearst walked. The immense frame moving forward was curiously light on its feet. He walked as if to music, as if somewhere a band was playing and he was advancing, reporting for a seat in a grandstand. He wore high laced boots. All the weight was in the upper body and the shoulders. The legs were light beneath him.

The executives had arranged themselves in two groups, one at each end of the room, and Mr Hearst approached first the left half-dozen men. As he went there, everyone in that area who was not in the group moved to another couch or chair, as small birds fly away at the approach of a big one.

Mr Hearst talked in a high soft voice. The day's news was brought from tickers; copies of all the newspapers were spread out on a large table. The King was very polite and quiet, and after a while he march-danced past to the other end of the room. Again the small birds flew away.

His head deserved the attention of the best sculptors and painters. The expanse of his countenance was almost twice that of the ordinary man—just as his thumbs were three times the size of my own. The most commanding thing in his face were the eyes, which were as large as fifty-cent pieces, but pale, like dusty stones, or like two immense tunnels running through his head. The nose was formidable, straight and strong, and occupying half of the big face. In profile it continued the straight line of the forehead. The shape of the skull, if traced by a pencil from the top of the forehead to the back of the neck, was a simple line, slowly curving.

The cheeks sagged and were grey. The face was most curious when he laughed. All its properties remained undisturbed—the sadness and the hollow eyes—but the strong jaw went down, the mouth split open, a relatively small and lipless mouth, and remained for a while like a half moon lying on its side. It was a melancholy lonesome laughter, but it belonged to the medieval man and was part of his design, like the instinct for moats, oubliettes, and towers, Gothic choir stalls and battle flags. It was all as simple as the stripes on the zebras in the landscape below.

The meeting on both sides of the room took about an hour; then everybody left.

For dinner, refectory chairs for eighty people stood along the sides of the table. Most of them remained empty. Places for the guests were prepared near the middle of the huge banquet table. There were place cards: one size for the guests, plain with the name written on it in a fluid hand; and a larger one with a gilt edge, on which was written in scrollwork 'Mr William Randolph Hearst'.

The Nuremberg-altar figure with the crown of yellow hair appeared, in black, with white starched apron. An old factotum, like a sacristan, lit the yellow candles in the twenty-five-pound silver candelabra down the length of the table. Two men put ten-foot logs on the fire. The catsup bottles were straightened out, and the condiments and the glasses of paper napkins. I thought of Elsie: there was nothing green and white striped here. The servants did as they pleased. This was another form of builders' and collectors' paradise.

The door with the laundry sign opened, and, with a draught of cold evening mountain air, the two dachshunds streaked through the room again followed by Mr Hearst. He passed through the hall into the dining-room and the guests followed him. The group was lost in the immense structure. There was the usual talk. The food was mediocre and badly served. The Moselle wine was superb. Mr Hearst drank beer from a very beautiful ancient glass mug. The executives sat with proper respect. Mr Hearst talked little.

Towards the end of the meal a friend who had travelled a great deal with him made a short speech. The little half moon in Hearst's face began to shine. In this controlled smile of his there were variations; for something that made him really happy—and it was always something back in the old days—he suddenly had eyes. It was as if a myopic man suddenly saw an object clearly in the middle distance and warmly admired it. This was a matter of seconds, then the gaze vanished.

The friend told old stories, and just as a child will listen again and again with pleasure to every detail of an oft-told tale, the sad King laughed and looked at the storyteller. The stories were of voyages, of difficulties with chauffeurs in the Dolomites, here and there, meaningful only to the people who had been in them. Occasionally a detail was wrong, a place not sufficiently identified, and then the storyteller was stopped and the facts reestablished. It was the story of an innocent voyage, never an off-colour joke, never an adventure in which everything did not come out right. Small misfortunes, mix-ups with happy endings, trouble that became immediately amusing when the traveller was identified or his generosity came into play.

Hearst's high voice piped an anecdote. His huge bison head wobbled. That again was uncomplicated, like the beer in front of him.

We got up when he did and followed him into the movie theatre. This was as grandiose as the swimming pool and the hall and the dining-room. Its ceiling supported by over-life-sized odalisques, the theatre held about two hundred people. Mr Hearst had a big armchair in the first row. The guests were seated around him and the help nearby.

A newsreel of the Teheran Conference was shown, and when Mr Roosevelt's lined face appeared the King remarked, 'Looks like a plate of tired whitebait to me.' A routine musical ran after that, and the evening ended with drinks in the living-room.

The newly arrived visitor gets very sleepy up here. The air is brisk and thin. I walked out on the terrace and around outside the castle. It was like Monte Carlo, but it was icy cold. A thousand white alabaster lamps lit it up, some of them part of balustrades and balconies, others standing along paths, along marble benches, next to statuary, and beside the pool.

I went back in and walked through the hall. People were playing cards. Mr Hearst sat with his eyes on the black peep-holes of the stereopticon and turned the images of his happy times. I left. I opened the door in the choir stall, entered the confessional elevator, and rode up to the Celestial North. I put my clothes on the black wire coat hangers and hung them on the candelabrum. The mattress of the costly bed was hard and cold, and so was the pillow.

I could not find the place to turn out the light, and left it burning.

The next morning I soaked my towel again and waited for it to cool, and then rode down to breakfast.

New trees were brought to the fireplace. In the living-room was a man with an immense aluminium pole at the end of which was a flexible wire cone. With practised skill he slipped the cone over the burned-out electric bulbs in the ceiling, then turned the pole until the bulb came out, and replaced it with a new one. An average of sixty bulbs burned out a week.

The grounds are vast. 'You really need a horse to see the place,' said one of the executives, who also had got up early and was having breakfast at the banquet table.

I got a horse a little while later, with one of the cowboys to ride with me. He brought the horse into a wide courtyard whose walls were unfinished, with the cement again bare, and the plain surfaces broken only in one place where an exquisite Florentine loggia was installed. In this courtyard, building was to be resumed, and antique stone lay ready in crates, to be unpacked, to hide the ugliness.

We passed the herds of zebras and came to a grove of tall trees. 'Those,' explained the cowboy, 'are for the giraffes. At one time we had a lot of trouble with them. We had two of them die on us and didn't know why. The local vet couldn't do anything about it, so the boss sent East for a specialist. A man in charge of the New York Zoo was flown out. He examined the dead giraffes' stomachs and found gravel in them. They had picked up the gravel as they fed, from the ground, and that was the trouble. Giraffes eat from treetops and can only swallow properly when the head is up high. So special trees had to be planted for them, but until those trees grew high enough we rigged up feeding troughs on stilts and pulleys that you can lower and then pull up filled with the leaves of those trees, and the giraffes are happy now.'

We came to the bear pits, which he explained were emptied at the start of the Hearst depression. 'They'll be back any day now,' he said with hope.

The paths go along ridges. To the west is the view down to the ocean, and to the east, always in a contrasting light, is an immense valley that reaches to the next ridge of mountains. Down at the foot is the village of San Simeon, with a post office and a general store where they sell picture postcards of the castle. There, also, is a dock where the ocean-going ships discharged their cargoes of antiques. There were warehouses with crated stuff, a railroad track, and cranes.

We rode up the hill again.

I did the tour of the castle after this, going down to the cellars—cold, cement smell, huge iron doors, double doors of black steel, large tombs. One held a collection of three thousand lamps; another of beds, pictures, chairs; others of tapestries and silver—an auctioneer's paradise of magnificent pieces mixed with junk.

I saw the custodian of some of these things. 'Oh, that fellow,' he complained of Hearst. 'I tried to get him to sell some of that stuff, and he promised me he would. Look—'

He took me to a refectory table on which stood a library of black-bound books, each made up of pages of photographs of antiques, their history, and the price Hearst had paid for them.

'I told him to sit down and mark what he wanted to sell. Well, he sat down here with the pencils I had sharpened for him, and he took the first book and opened to the first page, and then slowly he went through the whole book, smiling. I knew then that it was no use. He picked up the next volume, and he didn't mark a goddam thing in any of them, and sat there all day going through every one of them, always smiling. We needed money then, but now that fellow, he's richer than he ever was, and he won't sell a thing.'

One of the executives, who also spoke of him as 'that fellow', said, 'Christ, for five years, every day there was a crisis. We almost went into receivership, but that fellow never batted an eye—never said anything. Well, by God, it's the other way now. He's twice as well off. Now he'll start buying again, and that's good for everybody.'

The architect was one of the few happy people around Mr Hearst. In his shack were new plans, and there the King sat among models and on packing cases and plotted new additions. 'As long as he builds,' said the architect, 'he thinks he won't die.'

I walked with Mr Hearst and the architect along a two-mile stretch of trellised columns, fruit trees, and grape arbours. At one point Mr Hearst stopped. 'I want a terrace here,' he said.

It was a tough terrain, it would take a lot of underpinning

and work, the architect explained, and he made the mistake of asking the King why he wanted a terrace there.

Mr Hearst pointed to a scrubby tangerine tree growing across from where we stood and said in his high voice, 'I might want to pick one of those tangerines.'

'I'll never ask him again why he wants to do anything,' said the architect later.

I went back into the house. There was a message. Lady Mendl's secretary had called. Would I hurry back as quickly as possible? I tried to get the house in Beverly Hills on the phone, but the line was constantly busy, and the phones at the castle were all in the hands of the various executives.

A little later in the day I received a wire asking me to hurry back and signed 'Mother', and I was worried; but I decided to finish out the day.

I went back to the custodian. 'These things, of course, I wouldn't sell myself,' he said, pointing to the tapestries. 'I know the history of all the things here, of every piece. Outside him and me, I guess nobody cares a damn—not a goddam—for anything here. Now, his boys, they don't care at all. They used to run around here throwing things at each other, playing roughhouse among all these beautiful things. One time they had a fight with flypaper right here where the fine Gobelins are. They'd have taken scissors and cut the figures out like paper dollies if I hadn't stopped them.'

The telephone rang. The custodian answered. Shaking his head, he said, 'It's no use—that fellow won't sell them. He won't sell anything. It's no use talking to him even.'

He hung up and said to me, 'There's a couple of Chippendale beds that somebody is after, offering ten thousand apiece, but that fellow won't part with anything. Ten thousand bucks is just a dime to him. He'll never sleep in them—nobody else ever will. They'll just stand down in the vaults, just stand there until he dies, and he won't even bother to say who should get them. He doesn't think he'll ever die.'

An instrument of the very greatest epoch of clockmaking, its dial set in an elongated cartouche framed by acanthus leaves and marked 'Causard Horloger du Roi', struck the time. On the desk stood an abominable combination inkwell and ash-tray with a green nude, an arts-and-crafts objet d'art perhaps picked up in an auction room. 'Nobody is allowed to mention death in this house, but one day he will die just the same,' said the custodian; 'and God knows what will become of all this stuff that he loves as if it was his children.'

We stood at a window. The custodian pointed outside. 'And who will weep for Willy? Well, maybe the lame Duc de Bourgogne who rides through the cold California night outside of the castle, magnificently cut in stone, a falcon on his arm, grateful for having been saved from destruction in the bombing of his native land. Yessir, maybe tears will roll down out of those eyes.'

Early the next day, just before I left, Mr Richard Berlin arrived with his family. He didn't run away from the King and he had his own opinions, but out in the park he said to one of his little children, 'Now, dear, don't pick any fruit or flowers. Mr Hearst doesn't like that.' The child had an orange in his hand and explained that it was from the breakfast tray, and it was marked with the blue stamp of the grower. It was decided, however, that he'd better eat it right away. It was peeled, and we looked for a place to hide the skin. It was put inside a Grecian urn.

I took my leave, and drove off with many feelings, all of them low. I wanted to find a restaurant and console myself with the best bottle and a good dinner; but, alas, there is nothing of that kind in this latitude. I drove down the magnificent landscape, past the herds of animals silhouetted in the early sunlight, through the automatic gates, and it was like escaping from prison.

During the long drive in the blue haze of morning I came upon a truth, which, like all revelations, is simple as stone, and as heavy. I had met in Hearst the most lonesome man I have ever known, a man of vast intelligence, of ceaseless effort, and all he had done was to make of himself a scaffold in which a metronome ticked time away. Like Elsie, he had fled to objects. The revelation is that you cannot protect yourself, for you become desolate as the prairie. You must give yourself, you must take a chance on being hurt; you must take the chance to suffer from love, for the other is nil. In this visit Elsie was mirrored: the metronome ticked away inside a magnificent puppet. As lonely as Hearst.

I stopped for lunch at a modest place along the road. They had good dry martinis, and spaghetti and meatballs. Franz Werfel, describing a bad meal in *Class Reunion*, observed that even after the worst of meals a kind of contentment sets in. I drank a quart of California claret that was not bad, and some brandy that was awful. But by the time the coffee cup was removed I was in a tolerable mood.

I put the top of the car down and rolled slowly along through the beautiful landscape. A sadness came over me, to the point of stopping my own metronome from ticking. I had a feeling that Elsie was dead—I saw her as someone whom in another life I had loved.

I saw her the way one sees the saints in gilded caskets, their bones enshrouded in silks and festoonery made by nuns of jewels and silver and gold. It wasn't anyone who had really lived; it was a gallant soul who had borne the burden of an experiment in evasion and nothingness. It had been a fine time, a wonderful party. I had loved it, and it would never be forgotten. But I remembered it now as a mirage. My own face is, like all faces, the mirror of the world, and I look at it searchingly. The American painter Alexander Brook once asked me to sit for him. He works ably and fast. He put a large canvas on his easel, looked at me, and then started to paint; and when he was through he turned the easel towards the wall so that I couldn't see it and said, 'Come back again tomorrow.' I came back the next day, and he looked at me and wiped off the canvas what he had done the day before. He started all over; he looked at me and painted, and the same thing happened again. Then I came a third day, and after ten minutes he threw his palette into a corner and said, 'I can't paint you. The first day you looked like the messenger of God; the second day you looked like something out of hell; and today you look just stupid. What's the matter with your face?' I looked at myself, and I did look stupid; it was on account of a stupid day I had had.

During the time with the gay people I looked like something out of hell most of the time. The only time I was satisfied with my own face was when I painted, when I gave myself wholly to my work in the shack.

While I was living at Elsie's I read *The Theory of the Leisure Class*. I knocked together, or tried to, some kind of structure to explain it to myself. I said that not many people were needed to supply the necessities like shoes, coats, shelter, bread, and love, and the places and materials for those needs; and that it would leave a lot of people out of work if nothing else were called for. Were there not those who, by an extension of their needs, justified the talents and labours of artists, gardeners, embroiderers, pastry-cooks, and milliners? All this thinking led into a domain in which I was stumbling through unfamiliar landscapes. At any rate, I could see a reason for the existence of the people who moved in Elsie's circle, if only because they made it possible for travel agencies and suppliers of wine and fine foods to pay their employees. The people themselves never had a very good time—they hated each other mostly, and when one of the fine birds fell off its branch none of the others dived down to chase away the foxes of misfortune that carried it off and ate it.

The egoist loses everything. You cannot live for yourself. The pursuit of pleasure does not bring it. But all this has been said, and better—for example, by Bert Brecht in *The Threepenny Opera*:

> Ja, renn nur nach dem Glück,
> Da rennst Du nicht allein,
> Sie rennen alle nach dem Glück,
> Das Glück rennt hinten drein.*

I am reasonably steady in moments of danger, but I am a coward when other people suffer or die. I got hungry from unhappiness again, and very thirsty, and tried to stretch out the return as

---

* Yes, go—run after happiness!
You're not alone, you'll find.
They all run after happiness—
Which runs along behind.

much as I could. I came to a place with a restaurant that looked good; I ordered a big dinner, and it was very good. The plate was warm, and the wine was exceptional, a California dry white wine called Folle Blanche, a Schoonmaker wine, and it was clear, cold, and served in a decent glass. I found an excuse for further delay: I said a few kind words to the proprietor and I asked him where the chef was.

'Second door to your right,' he said.

It turned out to be the men's room; the proprietor had never heard the word 'chef'. I talked about cooks with him then, and he introduced me to the coloured man who had prepared the meal; then we had brandy and I drove on.

I passed rows of lighted cabins in which happy people lived. I passed along stretches of sea to the right, with moonlight turning it to green silver... I thought of the day when Elsie had made her will; she had become soft for a few moments, and I had forgotten it, because it didn't go with her portrait. Now it came back. In all the years of lonesomeness and discipline she had opened the curtains only once. She had dictated to West that day, when she thought she was going to die:

'When the spirit is gone, nothing remains. I want to be wrapped in a sheet and cremated.'

'Stevie,' she had said that day, 'you know the big lonesomeness, as everyone does who is like ourselves outside, and to us applies what is so beautifully said on Oscar Wilde's tombstone:

> And alien tears will fill for him
> Pity's long-broken urn,
> For his mourners will be outcast men,
> And outcasts always mourn.

'We are like corals, we build and the sea washes over us, and we build again, and the shells of our bodies become structure, and a new reef rises. And the winds howl over it in the lonely night. Most people don't know it, and they live satisfied lives.

'You know, Stevie, if I had a tombstone, what I ought to put on it is, I suppose, what I put on Blue Blue's tombstone, and Mother wasn't original, it was Willy Maugham, another lost soul, who gave me the words "To the one I love the best". I have sacrificed my life and myself—and I end up empty-handed. What is called courage can also be despair.

'You at least have your art, and that is everything. Give, don't take.'

It's too bad one cannot paint at night. I've never tried, but you'd have to light up your paintbox, or else flash a spot on the picture occasionally, to check. There is an American painter, little known, who lived in France and who painted very good night pictures. His name is Frank Boggs. I own several of them; one can buy them here and there in good galleries in Paris. I have an oil painting, a scene of the harbour of Honfleur, which has given me pleasure all the years I have had it. I look at it every day when I am in New York. It is in melancholy blues and browns, an old boat, a rope, nothing much and everything. There were the Boggs colours all about me now, and then came Santa Monica, and the road to Beverly Hills. I wished there were a few more miles. I did not want to drive up to the door. But when finally I got there the house was gay, there were cars outside, and then I heard the sound of a decorative orchestra, playing quietly. Mother was having a party, that's why she had sent the telegram. I was happy, very happy. She made all the faces, kicked me in the ribs, and asked for a complete report

on Willy Hearst, 'that wonderful *chk-chk* man'. I made him
out as being as happy a man as Mother wanted him to be.

The music was gay. I went and looked at my face, to check
my observations. I didn't look like something out of hell, I had
had a good time, and I had miscalculated. Elsie was not as
coral-reeflike as she herself thought; she was a tough old bird,
but she had gallantry, courage, and, like Charles, the gift of
friendship. I went down, happy to be back, and I drank until
Mother said, 'For God's sake, hasn't anybody here a home to
go to?'—which was her way of ending a party.

PART TWO

Elsie Abroad

18

Little Old New York

Mother was in New York at the old Plaza, which is a hotel filled with mood. It's one of my favourites; its candelabra, layout, and décor are garish in a *nouveau-riche*, gaslight style. Marble is piled on gold; the elevator grilles and all other hardware are bronze and solid, as if made for a stockade of elephants. There is a grill room of German rathskeller design next to a Louis XIV foyer. The chairs in the grill are leather-upholstered and made for the bottoms of the biggest men of the country. They were designed for the giants of another day; each is big enough to accommodate two of today's average citizens. I have to get up into them almost as if into a saddle. When I am seated, my feet are off the ground, and if I let my legs hang down naturally, I am so far forward that I can't rest myself against the back unless I almost lie down.

The chairs are done in dark umber-coloured leather, very polished from long wear, with the seats a little lighter in colour. The cushion which forms the seat is slippery, and it takes a while to establish a secure position on it; it's like Humpty Dumpty sitting on his wall. Charles approached these chairs

without fear. He sat solidly down in them. The air escaped
from the leather cushion. He leaned back; he was for once
comfortable.

'Good hotel,' he said, and studied the menu. He asked me
to suggest something.

The mood of the place was all for a solid meal. I proposed
roast beef. Charles said, 'No, thanks, I never eat roast beef
outside of England—only place they know how to cook it.'

Elsie was having a conference with the world's most gentle,
aristocratic, and able hotelkeeper, Colonel Obolensky.

'She's fantastic, the old girl,' said Charles. 'You remember
the floor she decorated at the hospital—well, she's doing a suite
here too. She's decorating the rooms we're in. So she'll send a
bill again instead of getting one.'

When we went back upstairs there were painters, uphol-
sterers, furniture-makers, carpet people, and Mother directed
everything. Marcel Vertès was doing some designs on the walls.

'Oh, I wish there was more time, Stevie! Mother would go
around with you and show you Little Old New York. Anyway,
tomorrow, keep the day open, and we'll have a look at as much
as we can. We'll go down and visit my little house, and have
lunch at Luchow's. We'll take a walk in Central Park and
afterwards we'll visit the Metropolitan Museum. Then we'll
see a play at the Empire. I don't care what's playing there.
I just want to sit quietly for a little while and look at the stage
and smell the old theatre. We'll start off at nine o'clock in the
morning.'

The next day Elsie came down in the elevator promptly at
nine. 'I'll order the tickets first,' she said. She walked over to
the counter where theatre reservations are made. An elderly

lady with pince-nez and bluish hair sat behind the desk, and in front of her was a customer.

'We've only got this one night here,' said the customer, 'so we want to see a good show. What can you recommend?'

The lady with the blue hair was going over a chart with her pencil, and she looked up after a while and said, 'Go see *Life with Father*.'

A woman who looked like a Wagnerian soprano had joined the line. She said to the out-of-town visitor, 'If you have only one night here, go to the *Walküre*—it's a must.'

'Is it that good?' said the customer. 'I mean, did it get good notices?'

'Notices?'

'Yes—what's it about?'

'Well, it's part of the Ring—of the cycle.'

'What cycle?'

'The Wagner cycle. It's an opera.'

'Well, you didn't answer my question,' said the lady.

The opera fan got a little impatient. 'Goodness,' she said, 'haven't you ever heard of Wagner, or the Ring, or the *Walküre*? The *Walküre* was sung when I was a little girl. I heard it the first time in Baltimore—standing room only. My dear father took me. He held me up most of the time. I thought everybody knew about Wagner.'

'All right,' said the customer, 'give me two for whatever the name is, for tonight.'

Elsie stamped her foot. She took the customer by the arm and said, 'Now, don't you worry a moment about not knowing anything about Wagner, or *Walküre*, or the Ring.' She gave the bad queen face to the Wagnerian. 'I know all about it. I had to sit through it as a child. I hated every minute of it, especially *Walküre*. The first act lasts a whole hour, and you can't leave. Go and see a good musical comedy. Have a good time. Go and see Fred Astaire at the Music Hall.'

The customer said, 'You must excuse me. You see, we're from Browning, Montana, and it's the first time we've been in New York.'

'That's all right,' said Elsie, 'just don't let anybody in New York impress you too much.'

We went out to the car.

'Here she is, milady—she's a sweetheart,' said Achille.

Mother loved green in all things except motor cars and clothes. In front of the Plaza stood a new Rolls-Royce she had ordered to take along to Europe. It was an eggplant-coloured town car, with basketwork, the type Achille called the 'To Hell with the Chauffeur' model. He sat out in the open. He wore a new plum-coloured livery and black gloves. The doorman helped Mother into the car, and it moved off silently, like a boat floating. At Fifth Avenue it turned up and into the park. We got out at the Mall.

There are two statues here, small and unhappily conceived; on the left is one of Columbus, on the right, Shakespeare. They have as much the Columbus and Shakespeare character as so many chocolate Easter bunnies, and they are dwarfed by two very fine seated figures of the Scottish poets Scott and Burns. We walked on to the shell where the orchestra plays on summer evenings. There is a bust of Beethoven facing the orchestra—facing the trumpet solos and *Naughty Marietta*. 'Good thing he's deaf,' I thought out loud. 'Now there is the man they should have put here,' said Mother. She pointed to the statue of Victor Herbert, who looks like the owner of a prosperous barbershop.

We went over a bridge and came to a small stone castle. 'Oh, look at the poor darling that wants to be a castle!' It stood there in grey stone, a little toy castle like the ones that come with tin soldiers. Some things were going around on top of its tower that furnish the weather bureau with information. We sat down on a bench nearby.

Mother had the mien of the general in battle. 'I'd like to be the Pompadour of America for just a little time, especially the Pompadour of this city. I'd get after the Italian, whoever he is, who is the mayor of New York. They're always Italians now, aren't they? Just look at the grounds! Parks are for people, and on a warm day people want to stretch out on the ground. Have you seen anyplace where you can stretch out and not find yourself in the middle of trash, garbage, broken bottles, and dog souvenirs? If I were the mayor of this town I'd take a walk once a week in Central Park. It's a nice park, but look at it! How is it possible for anybody to allow a thing like that in the greatest city in the world?'

'I don't know whatsamatter with them,' said the chauffeur, who had come to find us. 'They oughta throw 'em in jail or fine 'em.'

'No, Achille,' said Elsie, 'that's not the way at all. They ought to make this park so clean and beautiful that nobody would want to throw anything on the lovely grass. They ought to have grass like the lawns we have in Versailles.'

'You'd waste your time and money, milady. Them wops and Puerto Ricans and Harlem niggers, they like it that way, nice and dirty. I know. It's just like Naples. They like it filthy dirty—that makes 'em feel like home. They'd be afraid to step on the grass if you made it green and nice like in Versailles.'

A little coloured girl came by. She was very neat in a white dress, a ribbon in her hair, and she was eating ice-cream out of a paper cup. She was looking into the cup and almost tripped on the rough granite of the castle's parapet. Achille grabbed her, she gave him an impatient look, wiggled her shoulders out of his protecting grip, and danced off with the many extra motions with which small children move along. A few feet away she threw the paper cup down on the grass and ran down the stairs. Elsie watched all this. We were about to go when a squirrel came out of a bush. It picked up the cup and, carrying it in its teeth, went up a tree. It sat down on a stout limb, braced itself with its tail, took hold of the cup with its hind legs, and reached down into it with its little mouse hand and scooped up the rest of the ice-cream, eating it and licking it off its hairy arm. When it had finished it let the cup drop on the grass. Elsie shook her head.

We walked over a small bridge, where we met a man who greeted me by name. He had a sack hanging on one shoulder and held a stick with a nail on the end, with which he speared candy wrappers. He came to the paper cup and picked it up. Then he reached into his pocket and produced a paper bag. From this he poured some peanuts on the stone patio of the castle, making a sound like 'willy-willy-willy', which attracted birds and pigeons. He stepped on the peanuts, crushing the shells and the birds picked out the nuts. They did a quick job of it and then flew away. The street cleaner left the mess, said goodbye, and walked off.

Elsie looked at me. 'That man,' I explained, 'once was the night elevator man in my apartment house, and has now become a street cleaner. He has a daughter who goes to Barnard. He gets a good salary and is entitled to retire on a pension at the end of his service.'

'He's an Eyetalian,' said the chauffeur.

Mother turned to Achille. 'We'll have a look at my little house now.'

We went down Park Avenue, drove around Gramercy Park, and then turned right on Irving Place.

'Is that it?' asked Achille as he stopped in front of Number 49.

'Oh, my poor, poor little house,' said Mother and threw a kiss through the window of the new Rolls-Royce. She didn't get out of the car. After a while she said, 'I can't look at it any longer. Go on, Achille.'

The little house was dirty. In its basement was a tearoom; across the street from it, an immense building; to the right, a spaghetti joint and a garage; and down the street, the Irving Place Theatre, at which a film on the life of Leon Trotsky was advertised.

'Aren't we going to stop for lunch, milady?'

'No, I've lost my appetite… Oh, my dear, dear, poor little house,' said Mother. 'It had a soul, but I'm afraid it doesn't remember me any more. For twenty years it was my home. I shared it with Elisabeth Marbury. That little old house asked me the first important questions at the beginning of my career as a decorator, and I gave it the answers that made it a happy place.

'When I found it, it was almost as sad as it is now, but around it were houses, little houses, all of them friendly. It had a dingy entrance hall, like a rooming house. When I solved that problem the little house began to smile. I did it in a bright Chinese paper and grey velvet, and I replaced the dirty brown door with one that was made of small squares of mirrors, and that made the little hall double its size.

'With the first money I earned I bought a perfectly beautiful Louis Fourteenth sofa, and it fitted right in. The house welcomed it instantly.

'The house had one unfortunate thing about it, a bay window. This destroyed all the good proportions of the room that was burdened with it. I solved that problem by making one large flowerbox out of it. I had the floor tiled, and put plants in all the shades of green and of various sizes there, and I planted them in white pots. I think Mother can take credit for changing those awful brick-colour flowerpots to white.

'In all the windows I used white muslin curtains. That was a daring thing to do at the time. I had to fight those terrible lace curtains that always looked to me like underthings hung up to dry.'

We were now at the corner of Fourteenth Street and Irving Place. Across the way was Luchow's, and through the windows one could see the antlers of a stag. Mother leaned forward. 'There's another lost little house; it's interior has great spirit. We dined there Sunday evenings with Jules Bache.

'I met a client in there, a woman, whom Mr Bache was kind enough to introduce me to. It was at the beginning of my career. I needed business very badly, but she wanted to build an immense organ into her house, an organ of such proportions that it belonged in a church, not a house. When I told her so, then she wanted a piano, an upright piano. I must say that the designers of functional things have housebroken the piano, but the piano of those days belonged in the orchestra pit of a burlesque house. It was an abomination. So the deal fell through.

'Another thing I had to fight for was electric-light outlets. When electricity first came, nobody wanted to make use of it. Nobody believed that there should be light where you needed it. They loved dark corners, and tables cluttered with bric-a-brac. Well, I threw out the junk and cleared the tables of rubbish, so you could put the things on them that you needed, and I put light where you wanted it—for example, to read in bed—and a good bedtable that held the things you used.

'There was one more enemy that isn't altogether defeated yet, and that is steam heat—the worst enemy of all furniture. It ruins your complexion as well, and makes you bad-tempered. There is no way to control it except to turn it off altogether and be cold. There are people who keep the windows shut and the heater on, especially at night, and the same air is heated over and over again, and then they wonder why they are dead tired. Fresh air brings oxygen into the lungs, and this goes into the blood, so when you use it over and over again it's like washing in dirty water. No wonder they all look green and complain of headaches and have bad dreams.

'It's very hard to change these habits. Mostly they're stubborn and tell you that they've always had it that way and don't want anything better. There are some people that one can do nothing for.'

The car was now moving up the West Side Highway. An aluminium-coloured Alcoa ship was moored at its pier. We moved slowly in the heavy traffic, and people in adjoining cars gave us the looks of disdain and envy that go from the common car to the snob car. Only the occupants of a very battered old Ford, all of them Negro workmen, smiled with admiration and waved. Achille froze and looked straight ahead.

Elsie went on talking of the past. 'Good Lord, I was asked to decorate a house on Fifth Avenue many years ago. They were very rich people, and therefore top-drawer society of that day. The grandfather had run a ferryboat to Staten Island, and they were nice enough to deal with—but the house was hopeless. The hostess opened a door and said to me, "This is my Louis Fourteenth ballroom." I was so shocked I forgot my manners. I said, "Oh, is that what you call it?" Needless to say, Mother didn't get the job. That place looked like a gilded-furniture warehouse. They had fallen into the hands of unscrupulous dealers, who had sold them all the junk this Fifth Avenue château could hold. I read character by houses and furniture, the way gypsies read the lines of a hand. I don't have to see the person at all. It was a terrible time for houses.

'I will never forget a visit to Sagamore Hill. That was another place I could have done nothing for; it belonged to Theodore Roosevelt, and was out on Long Island at Oyster Bay. I suffered the worst agonies there. If you had to decorate a kaffir's kraal, or whatever a house is called in darkest Africa, you might try and remember Teddy Roosevelt's house. The heads of stuffed creatures on the wall, their pelts hanging beside them or lying on the floor, mixed with the weapons that had killed them. A foot of an elephant hollowed out as a waste basket, the skull of a wild boar complete with tusks as an inkwell. It all fitted together. He had done an excellent job of barbaric decorating for himself. I could never do anything for Rough Riders or big-game hunters.'

We were at Forty-second Street, moving slowly. A wave of gaseous fumes came across from Jersey.

'Look at this city, Stevie! How is it possible that man can make anything so ugly? Look at the neighbourhood around my own house, down on Irving Place! There's a little happiness left around Gramercy Park, but all the rest is terrible.

'You know, savages, once they have fed themselves and built a roof, and taken root, they then make things beautiful. The most primitive tribes created beauty—all kinds of beauty— none of it ever in bad taste. Now this is a young country, and you can't expect Louis Fourteenth to come overnight. But look—the streets are the same ones that served for traffic when I was born. Basically nothing has changed.

'There were giants who put rails across America and built cities; and it's finished, and the giants wither. There's no more for them to do; everybody has everything. And then comes a depression.

'Well, Stevie, you know what can cure a depression over-night? I give you the answer. It is to make America beautiful. Take New York! If I were the Empress of America, I'd order all houses between First and Second Avenue taken down, and on the other side of the city, all between Eighth and Ninth—and those would be the great avenues, planted like the Tuileries.

'And the Bronx I'd make into a Bois de Boulogne. It takes large measures like that. Oh, the dreams of the old days—the big sweep of the hand over little men's mean plans!

'And, oh Lord, what one could do to Jersey! Just look at it, and at that poor Hudson River, to have to die in such a filthy bed! Look across, Stevie! How obscene, how desolate!

It needs a Louis Fourteenth. Imagine if he had not done for France what he did, how Paris would look. Nobody would ever want to go there.'

'Louis Fourteenth, and Fifteenth, and Napoleon, and all the others didn't do it for France. They did it for themselves.'

'What's the matter with you today, Stevie?'

'It's just that the motive was a different one from the one you think it was. You love beautiful things, I love beautiful things. It's like with people who love dogs. They love to be loved by dogs. It's egotism. We do it for ourselves.'

Mother sat up very straight. 'And what is wrong with doing anything for yourself?'

'Nothing. It's the law of life.'

'Now, you listen to Mother.' She turned Voltaire, kicking her heel on the floor of the car. 'When I think about it, and I often do, I think about it in this manner: Louis Fourteenth was a creature of God, as we all are. If through his egotism beauty was created, then that was the only way it could be done, and that is all that is important!'

'Allow me, Mother, that the same holds true for ugliness, which grows out of economics. If it weren't for the stink of the Jersey flats, which comes from chemicals and glue factories, pig farms and fertilizer works, and for the ugliness of the riverfront, then you and I couldn't travel to Paris, and certainly Mother couldn't roll along in a new Rolls-Royce.'

Elsie looked out of the window, and then she said very drily, 'Well, I'm so grateful you're with me, Stevie. What would Mother do without Stevie explaining things to her? But you leave Louis Fourteenth alone! I'm a very old woman, and I tell you—and you listen carefully now!

'It doesn't have to be ugly. It can be serviceable and beautiful. It can make people happy to look at instead of depressing them, and the population of prisons and lunatic asylums will go down the moment people have a city they can love and homes that welcome them. I have never heard of anyone who had beauty around him murdering anybody or making anybody else unhappy. You agree, don't you, Stevie?' She kicked me so hard in the ribs with her elbow that I screamed.

'Yes, I agree, Mother.'

'I've never seen you like this before. Now, get back on board the Good Ship Hope! It's not all bad. Look up there at the beautiful span of the George Washington Bridge! There are people who believe in beauty—there just aren't enough. It must become like a religion, and I shall preach it and set the example as long as I draw breath.'

The car went down the ramp to Fifty-seventh Street. This empire mood was a new side of Elsie, and, like all emperors who are any good at their business, she let no detail escape her practical, sharp mind. We were stopped by an arrangement of things that looked like a Japanese funeral. The street was dug up, red lanterns were suspended from iron hooks, and striped boards fenced off an area. On high masts signal lights flashed on and off, and a very loud sign proclaimed: 'Sorry, dig we must, but we'll clean up and move on.' Under this was the name of the public service corporation.

'How stupid,' said Elsie, 'that sign! Up to now I always got mad at the government for tearing up the street. I thought it was the city that did it.'

We moved on and went past Columbus Circle. Back at the Plaza, Elsie stood looking out of the window of her room into Central Park. West asked if she still wanted to go to the Empire Theatre. The tickets were being held.

'No,' said Elsie, 'I don't think I want to look at any more of the past. I'll just think about it.'

At supper that night she said, 'It makes you feel old. I was thinking about the Empire Theatre. I played there in Charles Frohman's stock company, with Henry Miller—that's Gilbert's father—and with Forbes-Robertson. Mr Frohman bought a play by Sardou called *Thermidor*. I was the little girl that went to the guillotine in that piece. Clyde Fitch wrote a play especially for me, called *The Way of the World*, and there was another, *The Wife without a Smile*.'

Then she suddenly turned and said, 'Stevie, go home and take a warm bath, and come back and take Mother to El Morocco, and let's have a look at Big New York. I'm not a woman of yesterday.'

19

The Cyanide Pill

The apartment at the Plaza was finished. Elsie sat on the sofa in her drawing-room. Among the photographs on a stand was one of Grace Moore. 'Poor Gracie,' said Elsie. 'Poor darling Gracie, the way she went, in that airplane takeoff in Sweden. She burned up like a little chop. You know, Stevie, what happened to dear Gracie is never going to happen to Mother. Mother has a very good doctor friend, and she said to him, "Now, I want you to make me up a pill that will instantly and absolutely kill me, and I will take it in case something like that happens on a plane." And so he said, "Mind you, Lady Mendl, I wouldn't do that for anybody but you, but I'm dead sure you will never commit suicide." So he made a terrible pill for Mother, something like the one Göring took, and Mother went to her jewellers and had a little capsule made, of gold with some emeralds, and a tiny St Christopher with his hands holding the ends of a thin chain. This pendant has a spring lock that opens at the slightest touch, and the terrible pill is in your hand. Now, whenever Mother flies anywhere, she wears that pendant around her neck. So now we can take off and fly over.'

That night the doctor had to be called. Elsie was ill, and the doctor said that under no circumstances was she to fly. She argued about it for two days, and finally a representative of the United States Lines called, and arrangements were made for passage.

'I invite you all,' said Elsie. 'If we must travel in this antediluvian fashion, then let's do it in company.'

Dr Hauser had the good fortune to be in the room when Elsie made this generous offer, and he accepted with pleasure. He left to make arrangements for passports.

'Who else can we ask?' said Mother to West. 'We've got lots of room.'

'Well, not so terribly much, Lady Mendl.'

'Let me see the ship's plan, West. We have at our disposition a double cabin de luxe with salon, and two single cabins to the left. Then we have two inside double cabins. Now, where are we going to put Stevie?'

I said that the magazine I worked for, which was sending me to Europe, would buy my passage, and that I would have to see if I could leave on the same boat. In the next few days everything was arranged, and we left on the SS *America*.

We sailed in the evening. The morning of the first day out Dr Hauser took Elsie to the top deck, where he helped her do her eye exercises. He then held her as she descended the steep stairs and went all over the ship with her. Mother wanted to inspect every part of it, and she did it thoroughly on the arm of Dr Hauser. At meals we sat at the captain's table, Elsie at the right of Commander Manning. He himself was not present at the first luncheon; he stayed on the bridge. The afternoon was taken up with rest, and then a promenade around the deck, which Elsie did again with Dr Hauser at her side. He is a very tall and strong man. He had to walk stooped, and with very small steps, wherever he went with Elsie, so that he could properly support her. That evening the captain came down to dinner, and Elsie told him what a fine shipshape ship he ran. 'I'm a house-keeper and a decorator,' she said, 'and there isn't a loose end of rope or a speck of dust anywhere. I think it's perfectly wonderful, Captain.'

The captain smiled. Every captain likes to hear professional praise of his ship, and he said he had been a little afraid that Lady Mendl would be a difficult passenger. Commander Manning is a ship's captain, not a dining-room captain, and he was visibly relieved at her direct, simple approach. Now came the story of his life at sea, during which Elsie made her polite, not-listening face. She arranged various vitamin and seaweed pills before her, which Dr Hauser had counted out for her, and she took them while the captain talked.

'How interesting,' she said when the captain had finished his biography.

'So now I'm for ten years with this line, going back and forth from New York to Le Havre. My home is in New York.'

'Of course,' said Elsie.

'And in Le Havre I stay on the ship.'

'The ship is your home.'

'Yes, ma'am, it certainly is.'

Charles broke in, 'But you go to Paris occasionally?'

The word 'Paris' woke Elsie up, and she looked at the captain.

'Never been in Paris,' said Commander Manning.

Elsie put down her fork and looked at him. 'What did you say, Captain? Did I hear you right?'

'I said I have never been in Paris, ma'am.'

'The captain,' Charles said, 'has been travelling to France for the last ten years, and he's not been in Paris once.'

Elsie let out the old seagull cry, 'Ha!—what?' And then she said, 'Why not?'

'Because I stay with the ship, ma'am.'

'Oh, now come, Captain, you must have someone who can watch that ship while it stands still in Le Havre! Don't you ever have a day off? Don't you take a vacation?'

'Well, sure.'

'Then why didn't you ever get to Paris?'

'Well, I just had no desire to go there, I guess.'

'The captain just likes ships.'

'He certainly must.'

The captain ate the rest of the meal like a scolded boy. Occasionally Elsie looked at him with suspicion.

Later Elsie took Dr Hauser's arm, and he led her out of the dining-room and took her up to the salon, where coffee was served, and where he played gin rummy with her.

Charles said, 'I wouldn't mind at all going back with that captain. I know how he feels. Now, I like Paris very much, you know. I was in harness to my seventy-fifth year, and the post I had at the Embassy there was extremely interesting. You've got to have something to do in Paris besides going from one restaurant to the other. And now the world is becoming all restaurants, for people can't afford to entertain any more, and that is why these restaurateur chaps are doing so well. I say, what kind of a cabin do you have, dear boy?'

'It's nice—a single cabin with a shower.'

'Well, Hauser and I share a cabin, an inside cabin. It's not bad—the old girl should and must have her comfort. The other inside cabin is shared by the chauffeur and the butler, West has a small cabin next to Elsie, and the other they need for the maid and the pressing and cleaning that goes on wherever Elsie goes.'

Dr Hauser paid his losses and got up and led Elsie down to her cabin.

'He's awfully kind, Hauser, and fond of Elsie. Of course, she's the best advertisement he has for his regime.'

'What would I do without dear Gaylord Hauser' is what Elsie said several times a day on this voyage. Dr Hauser was with her all day and part of the night. Mother had trouble sleeping on the ship, and Dr Hauser was the only person who could put her to sleep. He had a small blue light which he attached near the wall, and when Elsie was in bed he turned out all the other lights and asked her to fix her eyes on the little blue light, and then he said softly, 'Sleep, Elsie, sleep. See the little black sheep, see the little black butterflies fluttering over black velvet, see the black sheep softly sailing over black rocks, watch the black frogs climbing out of black bogs, watch the blue light shining, the only star in the black velvet night.' Soon after that Mother fell asleep. Taking his little light with him, Dr Hauser left, softly closing the door.

The next day the boat was in a rolling sea, but Mother was a good sailor, and she made her promenades and came to lunch and dinner, on the arm of Dr Hauser. It was one of those third days out, when the day begins to resemble the one before, with the exception that the movie changes. The captain stayed on the bridge for his meals.

On the fourth day the monotony was lifted. A messenger came and asked me to come immediately to Mother's cabin. All the group was assembled there, and in a state of anxiety.

'But don't you remember where you lost it?' said Charles. 'Don't you have the least idea, Elsie?'

'If I had I would tell you.'

'No one must hear about this,' said Charles in Foreign Office tones. 'Not a word to anyone.'

'What happened?'

'The poison pill is lost,' said Charles, confiding the top secret to me. He turned to Elsie. 'Try and think back, dear—when did you miss it?'

'Well, I kept wearing it and forgot to take it off,' said Elsie, feeling behind a bolster.

'If anyone on the ship hears about this there may be a panic,' Dr Hauser observed. 'What kind of a pill was it?'

'It's a little pill, just like a sleeping pill or a vitamin pill,' Elsie said, looking around the floor. 'I wish you'd either find the pill or stop talking about it. I have worries other than this pill.' Mother waved the telegram she was holding in her hand.

'I'm going to throw all my pills overboard. I'll sit up all night in the smoking room rather than take my sleeping pill,' said Charles.

There was worried silence for a minute.

'The best thing is, now, not to trust to any pills that you don't know. In fact, I advise that all pills of any sort be thrown overboard immediately,' the Foreign Office said most gravely.

'Well, nobody is going to throw my pills that I paid a fortune for overboard. I have a year's supply,' said Mother.

'What good will they do you if by mistake you take the poison pill?'

'I'll take a chance on that. You hear, West? My pills stay where they are. Let Sir Charles throw his pills away, if he wants to.'

'You don't think, Charles, that we should post a warning or tell Commander Manning?' said the conscientious Dr Hauser.

'Heavens, no—he might put me in irons!' said Mother. 'And with good reason, I daresay. I think you're making a lot of fuss about nothing. Now, people don't take pills they don't know what they're for. If you find a pill anywhere, you or I don't take it. So what happens? It goes into the dustbin, the vacuum cleaner picks it up, it's thrown overboard, and that's the end of it. The fish eat it.'

It was left at that.

The day before landing there was another crisis. This time Charles sent for me as it was getting dark. He had taken his habitual afternoon sleep. He sat in his British underwear in his cabin and said, 'Look here, dear boy, what's just come by way of surprise. You know, she's really a wicked old woman. Can you imagine, she has the gall to send me a bill for my passage—and you know what she charges me? It's five hundred and forty dollars. Now, you know that's outright robbery. The minimum fare for an inside cabin out of season is three hundred and eighty. This, mind you, after inviting me. You were there when she said, "I invite you all to be my guests on this voyage." Now that is the absolute limit—it's an outright swindle.'

I walked into the smoking room and from a distance saw Dr Hauser sitting with West. He looked stupefied and then made gestures, like someone trying to explain the details of an accident—one that just happened, from which he had barely escaped. When I came to the scene Dr Hauser almost knocked his old-fashioned glass off the bar table. 'Have you received one of these from Mother?' he said to me, waving a bill like the one Charles had shown me. I shook my head.

He switched to German and said, '*Ach ja*, you are so smart you bought your own ticket. I wish I had... Now look here, West, all right, I'm glad to pay for the fare, but how does Mother arrive at this figure of five hundred and forty dollars—'

'Well, Lady Mendl—'

'Let me finish what I want to say—when other people pay only three hundred and eighty for these accommodations?'

'Oh, Lady Mendl figures the extras.'

'Well, I should say she does. What extras?'

'Oh, you know, Lady Mendl thinks in loose terms, but she remembers that she spent this for a telegram and that for drinks, entertaining somebody who got the reservations through, and a little gift for somebody else, and she tacks that on.'

'Good Lord!' Hauser groaned. 'A cabin like mine I could have gotten by just calling up the hotel porter.' He turned to me. 'I was invited. Elsie said to me, "Gaylord, you're my guest." But I'm just a butler. I haven't had a minute to myself. I take her up and down to the dining-room twice a day. She's taken over sixty dollars from me in that corner there, playing gin rummy, I always pay for the drinks. I am prepared to lose another ten bucks tonight, and I don't mind, but this is too much.' He fell into German again. '*Die alte Frau ist schrecklich.*' In English he added, 'There's nothing like mother love.'

West looked towards the door. 'Here comes Sir Charles. He's got one of these too,' she said, as if to console Hauser.

'Her own husband! Now that I can't understand at all.'

'I say, damn it, stop laughing, Bemel,' said Charles. 'I see you too have a bill, Hauser. This bounder got off scot free,' Charles said, pointing at me. 'What does this include, West, if I may be so bold as to ask?'

Charles put on his pince-nez and studied the bill again. It wasn't itemized. It just said in a bold hand, in green ink: 'Passage, $540.'

'Does it include the tips at least?'

'No, certainly not, this is just for the passage, as I have just explained to Dr Hauser, and for—'

'For good will,' added Hauser.

'It's for Lady Mendl's Public Relations Department.'

They looked at their bills and folded them. 'How is this to be paid?' asked Hauser in the voice of a loser.

'Well, the way you pay all your other bills, naturally, with a cheque on your New York bank made out to Lady Mendl, which you give to me before we get off the ship.'

Charles said, 'You know, I have an income of eleven thousand dollars a year. With that I could live in great comfort in Beverly Hills. I have a mind to go back on this ship with Captain What's-his-name, who has never been to Paris.'

He stared at Hauser and me with glass eyes, like a man who has been shot but is not quite dead yet. 'I wormed it out of the purser,' Charles went on. 'She had to send some money for that fantastic kindergarten she has started in Versailles. It wants doing over completely, and she says it's to be done right away; and they don't start doing anything in France, no matter who you are, until the money is in their hands. I daresay those wretched little monsters will make it impossible to live in the place. The one thing about it was that at least it was quiet. One could sleep there. I do hope she's going to put soundproofing into their place, but you can't soundproof the ground or the trees. It will rrring'—Charles always rolled his r's—'with their gay laughter. She's ordered swings for it, and every kind of gadget. That runs into money, and she didn't have enough along. This was the only way to get it.'

A page boy arrived and announced that Lady Mendl wanted to see everybody in her salon.

Mother was smiling. 'There's a problem about money,' Mother said. She had a bunch of money, beautiful French bills, pale blue and gay, in her hand. She said, I didn't know about the rule that one can't take more than five thousand francs into the country, and I like to respect the rules of foreign countries as I respect those of my own.' She handed each of us a packet of notes, amounting to five thousand francs.

'Now, don't forget to give that back to Mother when we're in Paris.'

20

The Villa in Versailles

Regardless of what travel agencies promise you, it takes at best three hours to get a car off a boat at Le Havre. The operation is difficult and tricky, and the work is done with care. The car is rolled onto a platform and hoisted by the ship's boom from the hold to the deck, then transferred to another crane based ashore that has a longer arm and more power, and this lifts it up high and moves it down past the side of the ship.

Elsie's Rolls-Royce came over the side, turning slowly, and then descended very carefully; and without a scratch it was wheeled into the customs shed. The third car off was mine; I had bought a small Studebaker convertible, which the butler was going to drive direct to Versailles. Half an hour after that the cars were serviced and matriculated with French plates, and we drove off. Mother had a blanket of grey wolf, and all the way from Le Havre to Paris she sat looking out of the windows, smiling at her beloved France to left and right.

Paris was deserted on our arrival. There were few cars on the streets. The police had put up roadblocks and were checking the papers of all automobiles. West had arranged for the proper documents, and we passed, and came to the Ritz on the Place Vendôme.

The square was empty, and the lights were turned on, the peculiar Paris municipal light of a golden-green hue produced by an old-fashioned gas stocking. The lamp gives out a sound something like that of a syphon, almost empty, being squirted into a glass—the last of the soda water mixing with air and going 'fhsss'. It's one of the details that make you homesick for Paris when you think of it. I heard it now, and the cosmic gloom sank down on me, as it often does in the happiest moments. There was the immense gratitude that the most beautiful, beloved of all cities still stood, and that nothing sacred and eternal in it had been damaged; and there was the intense sorrow in the streets. Everywhere on walls of houses small bouquets were fastened, and next to them were notices that here so-and-so had fallen defending the street during the last days. Most of the fallen were young people.

At the hotel Elsie stood at the window of her room and said, 'Oh, look, how wonderful!' Below, a detachment of Highlanders in their gay uniforms stood in the centre of the Place Vendôme with their band and performed the ritual of retreat.

The good hotel was cold, the elevators did not run, there was no electric light. The building had but recently been evacuated. Everything possible was done to make the guests comfortable within these limitations.

Someone gave Charles the address of a small restaurant. The proprietor waited on the guests and the wife cooked. There was an old parrot in the room, and he was very interested in Elsie, and whenever he looked at her his comb rose. The parrot was white with a little yellow at the tips of the feathers, and when the feathers stood up they looked like the leaves of endive salad arranged in a row. We sat close to a stove. The wine was fair, the food—as it is under even the worst circumstances in France—was good. The plates were warm, though the room was certainly cold. Elsie was in a trance, for tomorrow she would go to Versailles.

'*Ah, la joie de vivre*,' said West, freezing, the next morning. She had to receive and direct the placing of the cargo from the ship and the other treasures that were expected from storage houses. The French customs were most co-operative. The proper people had been notified, and everybody worked overtime.

The skies were grey, and the city, which, like London, wears its most shiny mantle of beauty in rain or snow, was cast in a grey light, with the lines of gold on its palaces and public buildings shimmering. It looked like a reflection in one of Elsie's mirrors. The Place Vendôme was brightened by the Highlanders as they climbed into trucks to return home. The Seine was high and fast-flowing; it had been raining all night. A girl in an American army coat, the only person visible, crossed the Place de la Concorde. A Frenchman was with us. He had acted as an overseer for the villa while Elsie was away, and Elsie asked him in French about the employees, the gardens, and the villa itself.

The Frenchman gave sage answers. He said everything was as good as one could expect under the circumstances. The chef, who was in his home town in Normandy, had been alerted and was on the way, the other personnel as well, and the maid, Eugénie, was out at the villa already, and so was Monsieur

Fleurtry, the gardener, and La Flèche and the butler (in my car) had arrived there early in the morning. All was ready for her ladyship to give orders and start things going.

His face was a long question mark when Elsie asked him how long he thought it would take to get the place in order. 'Ah,' he said, 'that depends, milady, on the good God, the weather, and the government.'

Mother decided that he was an obstructer and incapable of flight and imagination, and she gave him the bad queen face and kicked her coverlet and switched her attention to the scenery. We were driving over the bridge that leads to the Autoroute. The sun had come out.

Mother had her own way of driving to Versailles, and Achille did not go up the ramp to the Autoroute, which is the most direct route, but circled the rondel at the Place Clemenceau, cut left, and went through an elaborate golden gate that led up between stone balustrades and past fountains, through alleys of high chestnut trees, into the Forest of Saint Cloud. It was the beginning of what is called the Route de la Reine. Normally the gatekeeper extracts a hundred francs from those who choose to go that way, and hands out a very thin little blue ticket. The man there was so excited when he recognized Elsie that he saluted, forgetting to collect, and waved the car on.

We drove up into glorious royal-park scenery. The sun festooned the scene with a rainbow. The beautiful tall trees that line the walks glowed in the richest green-gold. It was spring. Then the black tree trunks came forward again, and it was cold and grey as the sun passed back into the low clouds over Paris.

The Sunday promenade of the citizenry of Paris was on, and the place was filled with drab, pale and hungry-looking people, hollow-eyed, holding their children close, pushing them in old baby carriages. Bandy-legged children too tired to jump and hop; a little boy with a sailor hat and a ribbon on which 'Invincible' was barely readable. People on crutches and in wheelchairs, many with limbs missing. There were some who walked alone and talked to themselves and to the trees, alienated by their losses, and panicky. Others gesticulated, playing pantomimes of despair with face and hands. Here and there was a shabby badge of ancient bourgeois well-being: a mangy red fox scarf, a faded velvet jacket, a hat with a wilted bunch of cloth flowers; a bent white-bearded gentleman in patent-leather shoes, cracked and with almost nothing left but the uppers. And all of them with big eyes, the bones in their faces showing, the ravages to their hearts and minds as evident as if lettered on their foreheads.

It was a Hogarth scene set in royal splendour. Part of the road was torn up, and the car advanced slowly. At the side of the road were pyramids of paving blocks. The people turned at the sound of the motor, then slowly made room. From their hostile expressions I thought it within the limits of probability that they might reach for the paving blocks and throw them at the car, with its liveried chauffeur and footman, which moved towards them as if mocking their miserable presence.

Elsie sat forward and waved her gloved hand at them and smiled—and, curiously, once they saw her their faces changed, and they waved and smiled back, and Elsie said, 'Who says the French are through? Look at them!'

Charles asked the caretaker about politics.

'Well, the Premier is honest but a drastic type,' said the man. 'He is trying to get rid of the black market. He's a brave man, but it's like picking up a red-hot stove with your bare hands. Any man at the head of a French government who is honest is lost, for he is surrounded by a carousel of crooks. They dance around him until he gets dizzy and either starts to dance with them or gives up.'

At the door of the villa stood Monsieur Fleurtry in the costume of French garden gatekeepers of the very highest category. It consists of leather puttees and a dark kind of knickerbocker suit made popular for wear in the country by Albert, husband of Queen Victoria. There's a buttoned-up waistcoat and a jacket with loose pockets. All of it was worn out but brushed and brushed again and especially pressed for today. He made his deep obeisance as the car drove in.

When we came to a stop at the door of the villa there was a small fountain at the right, and four large panes of ancient mirror set between rose-marble pillars. These mirrors had seven bullet holes in them. Curiously the shots had not shattered the mirrors.

'The Germans?' asked Elsie.

'No, milady,' said Monsieur Fleurtry.

'Who, then?'

'I beg to be forgiven, milady, the Americans.'

At the right was a small house, a sort of wing, into which West said she'd move with her kitty cats and puthy cats. They were not going to live in a garage in France. Ahead were the servants' quarters above stables and garages.

Inside the villa Charles turned up his coat collar, for it was icy cold in spite of its being June. But Mother took off her coat.

The villa was a battered, melancholy souvenir. A massive window at the left was patched with cardboard—not solid brown cardboard but thin stuff, parts of flower cartons that had arrived that day and had been hastily applied with tiny triangular pieces of metal which French framers use to hold glass in place before pasting the brown paper on the back of pictures they frame. An arthritic bug dragged one leg after him as he advanced towards a silver washbowl which had been placed on the parquet at a spot where all the polish had been washed off, and in this bowl the drops falling from above counted off the time. The portion of the garden visible from where I stood filled the frame of another window with the skeleton of a boxwood tree, which once had been artfully trained to resemble an elephant. He had had two white billiard balls for eyes, I was told, and when he was green the tree elephant sometimes swayed back and forth in the wind, very elegant and strangely alive.

The occasion was not without its ceremonial. A sad group of strays had clustered at the end of the room near the fireplace, some of them seated on packing boxes marked boldly: 'Lady Mendl, Villa Trianon, Versailles.' They were crouched there, dressed in old overcoats with the collars turned up, and looked like the substitutes in a football game made up of the members of the Académie Française, sitting on the sidelines waiting for their call. Two, indeed, had blankets over their shoulders and heads and steaming cups of tea in their hands. There was someone from the Legion of Honour, and other dignitaries from Paris. Near the fireplace leaned the mace of the official in charge of the reception.

All functions in France have about them a restaurant air, for there is always someone in a tailcoat with a chain around his neck, like a wine waiter. As we approached they got up and unwrapped themselves, appearing now in their various gala uniforms, seedy, and the gold on the cuffs, epaulettes, and buttons a dull brass. They stopped freezing, and the discipline of protocol took over; they smiled, got into poses of authority, and the phrases of official welcome started.

Monsieur Fleurtry took away the silver washbowl; looking apologetically at Elsie, he explained that this was from the last rain. The water now tapped on the floor, and Sir Charles said, 'For God's sake, somebody close that door!' Monsieur Fleurtry explained that the latch was broken and that the wind blew it open.

Then came the speech and presentation of a medal, in the free-handed French fashion of embracing and decorating each other on any occasion, and an answer from Mother, full of enthusiasm and gladness. The officials had a glass of wine and a smoke and decided to return to Paris.

Elsie went from room to room and touched the various wood panellings. She shook hands with the stair railing, and most probably she kissed the walls of the rooms that she entered alone. 'Oh, to be back again in this lovely, lovely house. Dear God, I thank you for this.'

The gardener was putting more wood on the fire in the salon. The wall brackets were down, some hanging by the wires. The electricity did not work. There wasn't any as yet in Versailles. The water wasn't connected. There were draughts everywhere. Furniture was stacked up under covers, and the men from the trucking firm were bringing in the treasures from America.

Elsie looked at West and was surprised by her expression. 'West,' she said, 'are you ill?'

'No, Lady Mendl, I am quite all right, I am quite happy.'

'But what's the matter with you then?'

'I was just thinking, Lady Mendl.'

'What were you thinking, West?'

'I was thinking how fortunate, Lady Mendl, that we are rich enough to take the next boat back to America.'

Elsie pulled her lower lip forward and made the worst bad queen face I have ever seen. She spoke sharply about how at a moment like this one needed support, and how the Good Ship Hope would sail through all this and come out happily. She saw neither broken window, nor wavy parquet floor, nor the unhappy elephant in the garden; nor did she feel the cold. She had her elbows out and her fists on her hips. She stood in her fighting stance, with the little girl legs solidly planted one here and one there.

'Elsie,' said Charles, pleading, but she did not listen to him. For once the butler gave Sir Charles the nod and moved over towards his side of the room.

'I am staying here,' said Elsie. 'Anyone wants to go, they may leave—immediately.'

Charles walked to the end of the room and sat by the fire. Old Eugénie, the maid who had stayed behind, the typical French woman servant, devoted to her mistress and willing to die for her, came in and fell on her knees and kissed Elsie's hands.

'Oh, milady,' she whispered, as Susan had done when Mother went to the hospital. Elsie raised her from the floor and asked her to sit down, which was the equivalent of embracing someone not a servant, and she asked in detail about Eugénie's life—her parents, who were still alive ('Praise the good Lord, milady'); her brother, who was a shopkeeper in Bordeaux and whose affairs were intact. All the questions that were important Elsie asked. Eugénie excused herself for wearing a shawl over her shoulders and a sweater, and another shawl around her head, and short woollen wristwarmers and overshoes. Mother, who was dressed as for a garden party, assured her that everything would be different now. She turned to Charles and said, 'There are some gifts in my bag, Charles dear. They're for the children of the Prefect of Police of Versailles. Would you be so good as to drive over and make a small visit there and leave these gifts, and then call on Monsieur le Maire? Or at least leave cards. Today he will be at home, not at the City Hall. West has a package of nylons for the mayor's wife. Ask them to come and see us.'

Things arrived from both the ship and a storage house. It got crowded downstairs. It was piling up with chandeliers in wooden cages, with boxes and crates and very carefully wrapped bric-a-brac and pictures. Upstairs it was altogether desolate. The rooms were hollow in their cold emptiness. Mattresses were rolled up. The plumbing was all that Charles had remembered it to be: very adequate by French standards, but unspeakable as well as broken; and the bathtubs were filled with crockery. The chairs everywhere were genuine antiques, but the smallest that existed of the Louis XIV style, and the hard wear they had been subjected to had weakened them, so that the legs were askew. It was all a little off centre, inside the house and even outside—the trees leaned, the bushes sagged, the trellises were twisted.

Elsie saw all this through the golden haze of hope. She greeted each souvenir, and her white gloves for once were grey with dust and dirt. She began to dictate to West. The work would start the next day, she announced. In a week she hoped to be able to have the place in order, so that we could move in.

Eugénie came in with a package wrapped in old newspapers. She tore off the covering and produced from it a golden unicorn, and she handed it to Elsie, her face radiant with devotion.

'I saved this from the Germans,' she cried happily. 'I hid it.'

Mother took the Cellini piece and held it close. She said, 'Thank you, thank you, dear Eugénie.'

Eugénie said there was something else, and from her pocket brought a dozen gold dessert spoons.

Mother took them, then handed them back to her. 'Here,' she said, 'keep them.' To make things clear Mother added, 'In the pantry, Eugénie.' As the maid left Mother's face changed, and she said, 'I wonder how many things were saved from the Germans that we shall never see again!'

West was directing the movers. They came in with an immense crate. 'This is not on my manifest,' said West, 'but it is ours. It came on the boat. I wonder what it is.'

'It's heavy,' said the men.

'Let's see what it is. Put it here.'

Elsie looked at it. It stood higher than it was wide; the signs said: 'Handle with Care.'

'I know what it is,' said Elsie, clasping her hands. 'You know, West, we were wondering if we had included the Clodion Nymph. Now, it is the one thing I can think of that fits into this box. Achille, get someone to help you open it.'

As the men got busy Mother said to Monsieur La Flèche, 'I saw a Picasso yesterday, an old blue Picasso. I wonder if we can risk it in the upstairs hall. That wall there wants something to look at when you come up the stairs. Monsieur La Flèche, what do you think about that blue Picasso? You know it; it's at that gallery in the Place Vendôme.'

'It's wonderful, but you know what he wants for it. He's asking twenty-five thousand dollars, Elsie.'

'But it's worth it. Let him send it out and see how it likes to be on that wall. Now, what have we there?'

The workmen had undone some bolts, and one of the sides of the box came open.

'Careful,' said Mother, pleading, 'please be extra careful of my darling Clodion Nymph—very careful.' The packers removed some pads that were like large comforters, cross-stitched and made of canvas, and then they came to packing paper... Mother stood with her hands folded, and she held them to the side of her face. The last protective covering fell, and there was Sir Charles's super-comfortable easy chair; the green leather still shone like new. It was in several sections. While Elsie looked on, the packers tried to assemble it. She did not find her voice to stop them. They worked, and then admired it.

Mother finally said drily, 'Take it out and bury it, or put it in the cellar. Take it away.' Before putting on a pair of fresh white gloves which Eugenie had brought in, she pointed out the door with the dirty ones, and she stamped her foot so the chandeliers tinkled.

West asked if the chair really had to go.

Elsie just pressed her lips together.

West said, 'I am very sorry, Lady Mendl, but, you know, Sir Charles hasn't really a chair to sit on in his room.'

'Has he complained about it to you?'

'Well, Sir Charles never complains about anything. He merely remarked about the fact that this house is only for small-bottomed people.'

Elsie crossed her arms and said with finality, 'One more word from Sir Charles about my furniture, or about small-bottomed people, and he goes back to the Ritz!'

21

The Kindergarten

Behind the Villa Trianon there was direct access to the park of Versailles. To the left, beyond the pool and a small temple and garden house, there was the usual kitchen garden, with a wall against which peaches and apricots, peas and apples, grew. The plots were hedged with apple trees, their heavy trunks dwarfed to a foot or two in height, but with branches as long as twenty feet. On these grew exquisite apples. As in most ornamental gardens of France, the fruit goes to waste and serves chiefly as decoration. The kitchen garden was sufficient to serve a household many times the size of the Villa Trianon; and there was a hothouse with some thousand flowerpots and wooden boxes in which pale green sprouts were starting to show. Beyond this wall, by way of a path, you came to a building that resembled one of the houses in the *hameau* of Marie Antoinette—deliberately rustic, with a pigeon loft, some hay in a barn, a few chickens—and all of it clean.

Hereabouts were the children of Mother's kindergarten. When I went there, I had the feeling of looking at beasts in cages outside a circus—animals that were being trained and would later be taken through the barred runway into the cage inside the arena to perform. Or again, they made me think of human beings that were to be turned into objets d'art. All of them were doubly orphaned. They had been recently transplanted from neglected, dirty streets and looked wilted out of their native habitat. They stood about in determined isolation, except for a brother and sister who held on to each other like two thin, ugly, suspicious, and very intelligent monkeys. It felt like the antechamber of vivisection, and the clinical mood was lifted only by the crib in the corner, where Wasserman Negative, Illegitimate Jones worked away with hands and feet, trying to get rid of his coverlet. He was a gurgling, happy baby. Half French and half Negro, he looked like a Houdon figure, terracotta coloured, with eyes that were a wet black and a face so filled with robust determination that one did not fear for a moment of his life, no matter what his fate turned out to be.

If Elsie had looked for troubled children, she had found unusual ones. They were the offspring of writers and artists, carefully chosen, and the one in his crib had the distinction of his colour.

The woman in charge of them was the concièrge type—fat, unimaginative, limited and righteous, and the warden of her domain. For the moment there was nothing to do here, for the hostility was complete, except for the occupant of the crib, who was now trying the difficult feat of getting his entire foot in his mouth. He had succeeded with the toes and was almost up to the ankle when I left, to the polite adieux and bows of the rest of the inmates of this institution.

I walked back to the villa. Elsie was busy; Charles had moved to the Ritz. West told me that my rooms wouldn't be ready for some time, so I got in my car and drove off. As I went along the road that goes via Ville d'Avray to Paris, I was thinking how good a mother Elsie made for me, and I wondered how good a mother she would be if milk was on the table instead of champagne.

The Zola-like realism at the kindergarten bothered me. I think that adult people have the right to do anything they want, if no third person is hurt, and that it is no concern of the police or the world how they amuse themselves in the privacy of their lives. To bring children or the defenceless into it is another matter.

I had a studio in an attic in Paris, and there I faced myself in the mirror, and I looked like a figure out of hell again. It was my conviction that my furious metabolism and energy, if not released in work, particularly in painting, would bring me to the violent ward, that my costume would be the strait-jacket and I'd find refuge only in madness. The kindergarten in Versailles threw me into the blackest despair; I decided to escape, and that also is a lucky thing—to have the desire to escape. I started to work on some paintings.

I have a dog, a *bouvier des Flandres*, which is a race bred out of the cart dogs of Flanders and those that herd cattle. They have lived with the peasants in their low huts for centuries. They are a rare breed. Although they look shaggy and awful, with formidable teeth and reddish eyes, they have the kindest and most patient dispositions and are perfect companions. The one I have is named Bosy.

I would take Bosy with me and drive out to the suburbs to paint. One day I stopped in Ivry and put up the easel. It was so cold on this June Sunday that I had to paint with gloves on; and the dog was freezing because the day before had been warm and I had had him shorn. I painted a street scene there.

As I drove back I came to a marker that said fifteen miles to Versailles. I had not seen Mother for several days, so I decided to stop off and show her the picture before driving back to Paris.

To drive from Ivry to Versailles by way of Ville d'Avray is not the most direct route but what Charles would call the 'pretty way'. By side roads one can pass through some of the loveliest and most curious scenery in France. It is a ring of bourgeois well-being placed around Paris. The parsimoniousness of the French is in great measure responsible for the many delightful things one sees. Like houses only half-painted, colours of several shades on a wall, repairs done by the owner with odd materials. The houses stand in little gardens, behind high walls and heavy gates, and not one looks like another. Individually they are monstrous and painful to look at. At close range and alone, each one of them is revolting, a poem of grossness, the dreams of butchers and barkeepers and small shopkeepers who have beaten the world and arrived at a respectable station in life. A hairdresser's secret image of architectural grandeur, expressed in stone, plaster, and iron without benefit of classical example or common sense. The most is made of the smallest of houses; they are castles with towers and moats, oriental palaces, Alhambras and Grand Hotels—although but two storeys high. They have round and oval windows, balconies like the Opéra, entrances as ornate as the Casino in Monte Carlo, reduced to a width of four feet.

Lit by the most awful lighting fixtures, and clogged with statuary and ornament, the walls of these houses are mostly invisible, hidden under décor. There is a garden crammed with ornamental shrubs and fruit trees, statuary, plots of rose bushes framed by pansies or forget-me-nots. Sand or pebbles are neatly poured on the roadway. The owner is busy washing his car, the children are seated somewhere behaving themselves, *Maman* is knitting and talking with a visitor. It is all precisely so on Sunday, in house after house, and the curious thing is that a good spirit exudes and a street of these terrible buildings, of which every one disagrees violently with its neighbour, makes a good picture. The best time to view all this and to pick a scene to paint is towards sunset, on Sunday. I drove especially slowly this Sunday, for I wanted to arrive in Versailles after dinner, just for a little talk with Elsie and Charles.

In Ville d'Avray I stopped at a petrol station and asked the attendant, in a white coat like a doctor's, to fill up the tank. He unlocked the pump and started the petrol up into the glass container from which it is released into the car. I had read that Balzac had owned a house here, and I asked the attendant about the house of Monsieur Balzac. 'Who?' he said. I said, 'Monsieur Honoré de Balzac.' He shook his head.

In France one always goes to the office to pay, and I followed him inside. He said, 'Monsieur Honoré de Balzac?' and very seriously handed me a telephone book. When he saw how astonished I was he offered to look it up for me. He repeated the name once more, opened the book, but could not find anyone called Honoré de Balzac.

I suffer an occasional compulsion to visit museums and such, but I am always relieved to find an excuse not to go, at least not inside. A locked castle or museum is a great joy to me. I drove on gratefully.

There is a very nice restaurant in Ville d'Avray, overlooking a pond that Corot often painted, and there I wanted to stop to eat alone. It is a robber's den called Cabassud, and it consists of a series of little huts, like the one Robinson Crusoe lived in, built of trees and matting, and in one of these cubicles you can sit and look out over the lake. The food is superb and the wine is good. There is also good conversation to listen to in the hut next door or below.

The robber took fifty-three hundred francs for my dinner and wine, and charged fifty francs for Bosy's dinner. But it was all very good, and I drove on, refreshed, to the Boulevard St Jacques in Versailles.

22

Old Friends

I rang the bell at the Villa Trianon, and old Fleurtry opened the door. He threw up both hands when he saw me, but not in joy. It had been a terrible day, he said; a great crisis was on, and Lady Mendl would certainly be happy to see me.

Elsie was in the salon, dishevelled, and with the bad queen face.

I asked, 'What happened?'

She stamped her foot and said, 'Charles invited some people.'

'I did not invite some people,' Charles said suddenly, out of a corner. 'You said that you wanted to see some old friends, dear, and anyone new that was interesting—and you asked me to do the invitations.'

'Well, they certainly are an interesting group. It breaks my heart, Stevie, to have to show this to you, but vandals have broken into this house. Wait until you see it. My dearest best service of Sèvres is irreparably lost.'

Coombs rolled in a tea wagon, and on it, on a large silver tray, were a half-dozen broken cups. Mother almost cried at the sight of them. She held up one piece after the other, and put each down as if it were a child of hers, dead and broken.

'Now, Coombs, bring those two poor little chairs. This is not all. I'm having an inventory taken. I am certain that some things have disappeared from this house as well.'

Coombs carried in two Louis XIV chairs. One had the right foreleg broken, a compound fracture, for the wood seemed very rotted, and the other had the entire backrest and back legs detached from the seat, and the seat ripped. The result of someone rocking on the ancient piece or leaning back too far.

'I will not forget them as long as I live.'

'Elsie dear, you came smiling, and you said, "Now, Charles, that the house is half-way in order, I want to see all my dear old friends and anyone new who is interesting, and I want to have a buffet on Sunday. Will you send out the invitations?" And you added—and West heard it, she stood right there—you added, "And ask a few extra people because, on such short notice, many will be obliged to send regrets."'

Mother looked at some broken china on the buffet and said, 'They certainly accepted. Oh, what a day this has been for Mother! At the last minute the buffet had to be enlarged and more wine ordered. As Sunday approached, everyone telephoned to ask if they might bring a friend or a newly acquired wife or husband, a cousin, a child. I think some brought their grandmothers. They were all people one knew in the old days, and it was impossible to refuse them, and when they came they descended on this house like a plague of locusts. They all ate like the Empty Stomach; the buffet was bare in a few seconds. They swarmed into the pantry and went down to the kitchen. The house looked as if an invading army had ransacked it.

Well, some are still here—go and take a look at them. They are not the same people any more—the clothes, the manners, the faces. The worst washed and combed, in sweaters, and some of the most neglected women I have ever seen, in slacks. Go have a look for yourself.'

I went into the salon with Mother.

'It looks like a Third Avenue thrift shop with people rummaging in it, and everybody hanging on the stairs like leeches, and all these extended arms coming towards me. Oh, and the Duke of Montmidi—look at him!—he's standing near the window, he looked like an old bellhop. It gets me all upset.'

'But there, Mother, is one who shines.'

'Yes, and she is exquisitely dressed, the Princess Paravicini. I shall ask her back again—and another, that lovely tall blond girl out on the terrace. Immaculately groomed and married to a sweet boy, a Roman count. What's his name—Gaetano something—'

Charles said, 'They're both American, these ravishing creatures, Elsie dear. The princess is from out West, and the countess is a New York girl.'

'Well, those are the only three people I asked to call on us again. They'll be here for dinner, Sunday next. Some of them seem to have gone mad,' she went on. 'That one with the straw hat—the kind Chevalier wears—that looks as if an old horse had chewed on it, he's an Ami de Proust.'

As he saw her look at him he moved towards Elsie. He was introduced and began to talk literature.

'Madame, Messieurs,' he said, 'I have written forty dramas in the last four years. Shakespeare is old stuff, this is new. In the last of my plays one hundred and eighty people are killed, not in battle or catastrophe, but one by one.' He asked Elsie to finance his play. Finally, for a hundred francs in cash, he made us members of the Amis de Proust. For another hundred francs apiece, he sold us a pin with Proust's name on it and his picture on the reverse side.

Another man approached. He wanted Elsie to rebuild his castle in Normandy and make a hotel out of it. Another offered her a painting of Pétain. Everybody had something for sale.

Mother smiled. 'Here comes Jean de Castellane.' She waved a little bouquet of lilies of the valley she was holding. 'He's the only one who brought something and who smiled. Not one of the others did. None of them missed the place or made a wrong turn.'

'They didn't come by car, Elsie. They came on foot, most of them, from the train.'

The last guests were slowly departing. Elsie said to Charles, 'Now, you know one only goes to places where one is welcome with open arms. I have never stayed anywhere where I was made to feel that I was not wanted or where I would discomfort the house and the service. If it's not that way, there is nothing to look forward to. Our world is gone—we might as well be dead. God knows I'm not gay, but compared to most of those who were here today, I am young and gay—*chk-chk*.'

It was midnight when they all had finally left.

'What is one to do about this? What has happened to all the charming people?' Mother asked accusingly of Charles.

'There's been a war, Elsie.'

'Will they come back again and call on us next Sunday? Charles, will you suggest something? I'm having a small dinner party. I have invited, so far—' She read off a list: 'The Maharajah of What-is-it?—Indoor or Outdoor?—and his current favourite; the Windsors; Paul Louis Weiller; that charming couple, the Chileans—what's their name? the Princess Paravicini, and that lovely young couple Count Gaetano Something and his American wife... That makes us thirteen at table. Well, we'll find somebody else. Now how about those others, Charles? The locusts, if they come again, what will we do? There must have been at least a hundred who were not invited at all.'

'They were always welcome here before. I knew almost everyone personally.'

Elsie stared into the fireplace. 'I seldom trouble you, Charles, but in matters like that I depend on you to find a solution. Give me a good solid British piece of advice.'

'I'm afraid I can't help you, Elsie, at least not with a British piece of advice. You see, in England, no one sends out invitations to a party like this nowadays, and if they were sent, few people would accept, for very few could return the hospitality of your house. So let's leave England out of it. As for France— well, you can send fifty pounds to a fund for broken-down aristocrats and ease your conscience that way, and turn your back on them.'

'I've asked for a solution, Charles, not a sermon.'

She wore the worst bad queen face.

'Well, frankly, I would open a soup kitchen, and call it a buffet, in a tent in the garden on Sundays, and feed them. I'm certain the duke wouldn't mind, and everybody would have a wonderful time. They were always so bored when they were stuffed and bloated with food and wine.'

Mother let out the seagull cry. 'Ha! All right, Charles, I'll hire the upstairs of Maxim's, Sunday nights, and call it a buffet supper, to ease my conscience, as you put it. You don't seem to understand what I'm driving at—you've seen what they did to the house. Can you imagine what they'll do to the garden?' She turned to me. 'Stevie, listen to Mother. When an artist draws a bad line he rubs it out. And when you have put the wrong colour on paper you tear the paper up. And something that belonged to yesterday is out of fashion today. And sometimes decisions are hard to make, but they have to be made.'

She looked at the broken porcelain and the broken chairs as if she were a judge looking at the evidence in a murder case. 'I'm still waiting for a solution, Charles.'

Charles looked the way he did when she had gone off to the hospital. He was tired and old, and he lifted both his shoulders and dropped them again; and, folding his arms, he looked out through the high glass doors into the dusk.

'I don't know what to tell you,' he said. 'I tried to tell you in Hollywood. But you don't listen to me.'

Mother called the butler and sent for Monsieur Fleurtry, the gardener.

'Monsieur Fleurtry,' said Elsie, 'I have something to ask you which demands the greatest tact and savoir-faire.'

Monsieur Fleurtry, who was, in spite of his advanced years, known as the Satyr of the Boulevard St Jacques, made a courtly bow and gave a look of immediate and deep understanding, thinking he was to become part of an intimate and romantic plot.

'Come closer, Monsieur Fleurtry,' said Elsie, with a smile, the smile she had for servants, disciplined as was all the rest of her behaviour.

Monsieur Fleurtry bent down to her, maintaining a respect-ful distance.

'Charles, what is padlock in French?'

'*Un cadenas.*'

'Well then, Monsieur Fleurtry, I shall order a *cadenas* to put on the gate of the villa, and we will lock the door next Sunday. But that doesn't mean that everybody will be kept out. Here are the names of the people on the dinner list. Whoever is on it will be allowed to come in; the others not.'

Fleurtry looked at the list and said hopelessly, 'Oh, milady, I have a terrible memory for names. All these names—I will certainly not be able to keep them in my head.'

Mother was thinking hard. 'Very well,' she said. 'Then this is what we shall do. I will give you the guest book, and you will be at the door, and when anyone approaches, you will say the following: "Monsieur"—or "Madame"—you will say, "Lady Mendl is very ill. The doctor has said that she cannot see more than two or three people a day. She must have complete rest. But will you please sign your name in this book so that she may know who was so kind as to come and see her."'

Fleurtry held his cap in both hands and turned it slowly, like a wheel that steers a small boat.

'Do you understand what I am saying?'

The gardener nodded.

'Now, after they have signed their names in the book, Monsieur Fleurtry, you look at the name, and if it is one of the names of the people we have invited, you say, "Pardon me, but you are expected."'

'And then shall I let them in?' asked the gardener.

'What is worrying you, Monsieur Fleurtry?'

'The names of the guests, which I shall not fail to forget.'

'That will be very easy. We shall paste a list of them on the inside of the cover of the guestbook, and you can take a look there and check the names. That is all, Monsieur Fleurtry.'

Charles said, 'You know, poor Fleurtry has been here a long time. He's getting on.'

'Well, it's as simple as ABC, Charles. He stands there at the gate, there's a lantern overhead, giving plenty of light, he can see well enough to read, he has it all written down for him, and all he has to do is to see that the name of the person is on the list.'

Elsie went up to her apartment. Charles and I walked down through the park to the garden house that faced the pool. Down there I had some cigars in a closet, and a bottle of brandy; there was an icebox and glasses, and we sat in wicker chairs and watched the blue smoke of the cigars drift over the water and rise upward in shreds, for the water was warm from the heat of the day and the air about it cool.

After a while West came. She carried a box filled with broken glass and china; she was going to put it in the refuse cans at the end of the house so that Lady Mendl wouldn't come upon it again.

The kindergarten was dark and silent.

'Very well behaved,' said Charles.

'Lady Mendl is there every day,' said West.

'Is it so long ago that we left here?' Charles said, looking at the broken things.

'Well, four years, Sir Charles, but then, you can't blame Lady Mendl altogether. You know, they got the rugs and the wallpaper dirty. Half of the things that happened I didn't even tell her. Twenty-three demitasse spoons are missing, and three forks. And the little Fabergé clock.'

'By the way, how is the old girl? Has she gone off to sleep?'

'She's up there making arrangements for some fireworks on the fourteenth of July.'

'Tomorrow night I'm dining out, West.'

'Well, Sir Charles, have a good time. I envy you.'

'Oh, I wish I could say that to you, but I pity you.'

'You may well, the worst is yet to come. I have some very bad news from the treasury for milady. The figures are all in black. She's spending far too much money on the kindergarten and on this house.'

23

Thirteen at Table

The damage done on Sunday was repaired. The carpets were thoroughly cleaned, the walls washed, and the wallpaper carefully restored. Monsieur La Flèche had engaged extra help, and painters were busy on scaffolds, freshening up the magnificent ceiling of the dining-room. This was one of the happiest and most successful rooms conceived by Lady Mendl.

It was a room resembling a tent built according to her design. It was of pale green and with a ceiling of green and white stripes. She had immense panes of glass placed so that there was the illusion of dining outdoors. On the side towards the house the room took on solidity, with statuary, a platform for the orchestra, and room for the reception of the guests and for coffee after dinner. It was like a most elegant private restaurant, well thought out, efficient, and gay.

The dinners were exemplary and simple, and the rules laid down for the serving of meals were sensible. The basic laws were a cool room and hot plates, the floral decorations low, so that one could look across at the other people and talk to anyone without bending around a vase or candlesticks. Her love of

things green and white went so far that the place cards were
tropical leaves on which the names were written in white ink.
The lighting was indirect and the service the ancient Russian,
which is the most convenient for the guest at table as well as
the help. It consists of a small rolling table, or, in the case of
larger parties, of several of them. The food and the plates are
placed thereon, and the servitors arrange the food on the plate
and set it before the guest.

Since there was always a small green and white menu at
the table the people knew what was coming, and they could
choose more of the first course, if they liked that, or more of
the second, if that course had more appeal to them.

The French service, the passing of the heavy silver platters,
is awkward. Not infrequently the butler and footmen are hot
and perspiring. They break up conversations as they lean down
between people, passing the food. Frequently things are spilled.
This style of service is not too easy on either guest or attendant.

I have never known any hostess, hotel manager, chef, or
maître d'hôtel who gave the attention to a party that Lady
Mendl did. It started with an inspection of the room, with
searching for dust with the white gloves. With acquainting
herself anew with the chef and his problems. With seeing
to the reception. That is, checking who received the guests
and helped them from their cars, who opened the door
for them, who took their coats, who showed them into the
salon. She went over every detail of the service, and in the
case of people whom she had not met she informed herself
about them.

On that Sunday, dinner was especially important, for it
was the first to be given there since the war. To Charles it

was a serious matter, for the man who had been his King was coming to dine.

A decorative orchestra played softly behind a screen of greenery. Mother was the queen again, and she pulled at her gloves as she sat waiting; for it was nine, and then nine-fifteen, and not a single guest had appeared.

Sir Charles looked at his watch. The butler said, 'Traffic in Paris, milady, is now as bad as in New York. And besides, the petrol is awful.'

The butler and chauffeur had permission to talk when Mother was alone, that is, with the family but without guests present. Sir Charles did not grant this licence except to his man John, and he objected to servants making conversation beyond 'Yes, sir' or 'Yes, Sir Charles'. On evenings like this Achille hired somebody to do the receiving and opening of car doors outside, and he, in livery, stayed inside, close to Lady Mendl.

'They're all late on account of the petrol, milady,' he began. 'Now the other night, sir, for example, I put three filters on this Rolls, paid for out of me own pocket, and still, on the Autoroute, the car jerks, and the motor starts fading on me. So of course I know what the trouble is. It's the petrol. There's stuff floating around in this petrol that's like the skin off boiled peaches. Well, I picked it out of the filter. But here we are on the Autoroute, and I have Lady Mendl alone in the car, and she's loaded with jewels: she's wearing the big diamond and emerald collar, the Indian necklace, and two sets of bracelets. We're a target—know what I mean, sir? Well, I always carry that gun, my thirty-two automatic, but what good is it when I'm under the hood of the car, working on the motor? Any time a guy is under the hood of a car, especially at night, he's a cinch for a target. So I kept coming up to see if milady was all right, and I had the gun right there, laying on the motor.'

Elsie said, 'Now, just think, Achille worrying about all these things and protecting Mother! He really cares. There aren't many who do. I had no idea there was any danger. I was looking over in the direction of Versailles, enjoying the glow that hung over it. That was very good of you, Achille.'

'Don't mention it, milady.'

Charles looked at his watch.

'I'm glad that nothing happened. After I got all that stuff out of the carburettor she started again, and we went off.'

Achille stopped talking, for the gardener had come in. He was smiling and carried a huge bunch of roses in his arms. He had his cap in hand and asked, 'Where shall I put these, milady?'

'Who sent them?' asked Mother.

'Some people, they brought them, and then they signed the book and left.'

Mother screamed. 'What? Where is that book, Fleurtry?'

He had it under his arm. She looked at it and cried, 'That fool has sent everyone away. Here are the signatures.'

Elsie stood up and read in trembling voice, 'Edward and Wally, we hope you get well soon; the Maharajah of Indore; and dear Paul Louis Weiller who has been so kind and generous, he was sent away too.'

There are engravings showing generals standing on hills, surveying the scene of lost battle, in wind, and with rain beating in their faces. That is what Mother reminded me of as I looked at her that evening.

The butler was studying the guest book.

'Has he sent everyone away?' Charles asked hopelessly.

'Well, not exactly, milady,' said the butler. 'The others seem to be late.'

'Well, run and open the gate and let the people in, for heaven's sake. Let in anyone who comes.'

Charles looked like another general of lost battle.

A car rolled in; it was the young couple, the American wife with the Italian count. They were both tall, handsome, young, and busy with excuses for the delay.

Another car rolled up. It was the princess, who wore jewels up to her elbows and had her throat encased in a diamond choker higher than that of the hostess. She wore a large hat with bird-of-paradise plumes, and immense rings and a string of pearls that was tied like a rope. She looked like one of the stars from the Folies Bergère, except that she wore clothes under her jewellery.

The footmen were busy rearranging the table. It was all done quietly and efficiently. They had taken off some covers and replaced the cards. Sir Charles had placed the princess to his right and the countess to his left. The music was playing, and the cocktails were being handed around.

Monsieur Fleurtry appeared at the door again, smiling; he held up two fingers. 'Two more,' he sang in his croaky voice, and in came two people who were in country clothes.

Lady Mendl smiled and extended her hand. The man was heavyset and ruddy, the woman a purposeful, sharp-eyed person, with reddish hair and another hue of red on her cheeks. She had the air of the easily irritated, and she also wore a great deal of jewellery with her suit.

'We happened to drive by, and we saw light in your windows,' the man said to Sir Charles, slapping him on the back. 'So we thought we'd drop in.'

'Have you had dinner?' Lady Mendl asked, with the hope that they had eaten and just dropped in for a drink.

'Well,' said the man, 'we had a snack, but if this is an invitation I accept it with pleasure.'

In a moment the room echoed to the happy laughter of the new arrival. He told jokes—not Mother's kind of jokes.

Smiling, she detached herself after a while and took Charles aside. 'Who are these people?' she asked.

'That is the Empty Stomach and his wife,' said Sir Charles.

The lowest comedian of a provincial stock company could not have done greater justice to the role the Empty Stomach played. He impersonated a comical pig at table. He stuck the napkin into his collar. He monopolized the conversation, speaking mostly of himself and his wife, to whom he referred as 'the Missus'. He buttered himself a roll—cutting it in half, holding one half in his hand and going back and forth over it with the knife and all the butter that was on his butter dish. His great weight almost collapsed the delicate chair on which he balanced himself.

The servants exchanged silent glances, and Elsie sat sideways at her place and watched the Empty Stomach. He looked at her and smiled jovially.

Elsie smiled back and asked, 'What's your favourite dish? I hope we have something you like on the menu for tonight.'

'I have no favourite dish. I'm not interested in eating,' said the Empty Stomach. The butler had just placed a cup of vichysoisse before him.

'Oh, come now,' said Mother. 'We all know that you are a great gourmet. Do you like duck? We're having duck with wild rice tonight.'

'Hm-hm,' said the Empty Stomach. He had just lifted the frail cup to his lips, very elegantly, with both fat pinkies sticking out. He drank the soup like beer, then wiped his mouth. 'How about you, Lady Mendl? You're not a vegetarian, by chance?'

'Oh no, I like meat. What kind of meat do you like, Mr Munchin?'

'Well, I tell you frankly, intelligent animals I don't like to eat. For instance, I'd say that a duck is stupid—he has only one sound, *quack, quack*; and lobsters are dumb, and so are fish. But pigs, that's something else. I don't like to see a pig on the table, I find pigs quite human.'

'I know exactly what you mean,' said Elsie.

'The rest I like.'

'What do you like most?'

'Well, I like most a full portion of everything.'

A vol-au-vent of langouste came next, and the Empty Stomach said that he did not object to the langouste, this animal being in a class with lobster, and he dug in as if he were a mason trowelling cement on bricks. It was gruesome to watch him shovel the food. He held the napkin up over his chin so he wouldn't get any of it on himself. The white of the plate came through the sauce, which he mopped up with a piece of bread, explaining that that was the way one ate in France.

Elsie placed her napkin in front of her and said, 'Forgive me, but I don't feel at all well. I think I must leave you.' She got up and nodded to all, and then on the arm of Sir Charles she went up the stairs. The princess waved after Mother. She seemed to have been to several cocktail parties before she came to the house. She gave everyone a wide smile and said hello to each person as if they had just come in.

The princess turned out not to be an American; she only loved America. She had been married to three Americans before she became the princess. She was Hungarian by birth.

The Empty Stomach sat next to her and admired her jewels. He pointed with an extended fat finger at the emerald on her right hand and said, 'What a lovely stone!'

'Das is nozhing,' said the princess, showing him one double the size on her other hand. 'This one is insured for half a million dollars.' She laughed a shrill laugh.

The Empty Stomach looked at her pearl necklace. 'These are all perfectly matched,' she said. He picked up the rope and held the pearls in his hand. 'You vant to see it?' she said, and pulled at the string. It came off and lay on the table. She grimaced again and sent her wide, fixed smile around the table.

Suddenly she screamed, 'The clasp, the ruby clasp!'

The service stopped and everybody was silent.

'Nobody leaves this room,' said the princess.

Sir Charles stood up. 'I say,' he began, but she cut him off and, slowly waving a finger at him, repeated, 'I said, nobody leaves this room.'

'Now, listen here, maybe it broke off and slipped down your back,' said the Empty Stomach.

'Maybe it did,' said the princess.

She turned and motioned to the nearest footman to come close, and she pointed down the back of her dress. 'Go on,' she said. 'Go and see if it's there. Don't be afraid.'

The footman, who was young, blushed and looked at Sir
Charles with his large, sad, French eyes. Charles had a habit
of closing his eyes and nodding when he had to approve of
something he did not approve of. He nodded. The footman
approached and put his gloved hand down the back of the
princess. He came up with nothing and was happy to return
to his place against the wall.

The Empty Stomach was on his knees under the table,
and he rose with the clasp held in his hand. It had been on
the carpet.

'So you found it,' said the princess, giving him a long look
with raised eyebrows. She lifted a glass and sipped slowly, her
nose in the glass; she looked over the rim at the young Italian
count, who had been laughing through the entire séance so
that tears ran down his cheeks.

'Funny, eh?' said the princess.

'Yes, very funny.'

'What are you? I mean, where did you come from?'

'Italy.'

'Oh, a wop.'

'Yes, a wop, what's wrong with wops?'

'Wops make lousy soldiers, that's what Jack used to say.'

The countess came to her husband's aid. 'Yes, maybe they
make lousy soldiers, but because a guy isn't a good tennis player
doesn't mean you can't love him anyway.'

'Jack was my first husband,' said the princess, and then she
collapsed and the chair fell on its back with a broken leg as she
slid under the table.

The Empty Stomach turned gallant. He helped the butler
to take the princess to a couch in an adjoining room.

The service continued, and again a cover was removed from the table. Until the dessert there was sober and proper conversation, as if Mother had been at the table.

When everybody got up, the wife of the Empty Stomach came over to Charles and said, 'I want to ask you something. Maybe this would interest you. We're going to live in France. I like it here, I love service and good food, but we don't know anybody here. Now, I always think the best way to solve a problem is to meet it head-on. So I make you an offer—I pay you a thousand dollars a month and you take me to places, like Maxim's, and introduce me to a few people.'

Charles stared at her.

'Besides, I take care of the bills, naturally, whenever we go out.'

'How dare you ask me anything like that?' said Charles.

'Well, I thought you could use the money. I just thought it was a good idea, and if you ever change your mind the offer still stands, and no need to get sore about it.'

Charles looked as if he also had to go up to bed.

The butler came and offered brandy. The wife of the Empty Stomach went to look after the princess, and the men sat together.

The Italian was conscious of the misery Charles was in, and, with the great gift for compassion of his race, he pulled hard to make the atmosphere gay. He sensed that Charles was not in the graces of Elsie at the moment and that his evening had been ruined, and he tried to console him with the dilemma of being married to an American woman.

'Oh, Evie—I love her, but she makes my life one long inferno. What they can do to you, American women! I gave up. I decided, right after we were married, not to fight. The princess is right. We make lousy soldiers because we have too much imagination, that's why.'

'I'm very sorry,' said Charles.

The Empty Stomach said, 'That was a fine dinner we ate tonight.'

'Sir Charles, I must tell you about Evie and me,' said the count, pulling his chair closer. 'My wife, you know, Evie— well, there is that business of eating in various countries. We are married and we go to my mother's in Rome and Evie eats. You know Americans, they cut everything up first and then they put the knife away and put the fork in the knife hand, and they push the peas to the right and the potatoes that way, and then they pick the meat up, and with the other hand they hold up the chin and put the elbow on the table. Well, my mother looked at me, and at the other people at table, and then her eyes pointed at how Evie was eating, and everybody watched her. So after we got home I said, "Look, darling, if we live in America I would go out of the house in the morning with dirty shoes and step on a chair and have them shined, because that's the way you do it there; but here I have a valet who shines my shoes. We're living in Rome, and when in Rome, do as the Romans do. So please eat like a Roman, using both hands, the fork in the left, the knife in the right."

'That was the first fight, and you know how it ended. I eat now with the fork in the other hand, and half of Rome does. All the young people copy it. And then that other business, oh *Dio mio*! One day she says to me, the way you say, "Please get me a pack of cigarettes," she says, "Darling, I am not well.

Will you go out and buy me a box of those things, you know what I mean."

'"What?" I said. "I go out and buy that?"'

'She said, "Yes, go on and hurry up, I want to get dressed."'

'I said, "Well, in Italy that is not done."'

'So she said, "Shut up, and buy it."'

'So we have an argument, and I hate arguments, and of course I go out. So I pass this *pharmacia* six times before I go in. Finally I go in. A man with a beard comes—he looks like my papa—and says, "What is it you want?" I say, "Aspirin," so he gives me aspirin, and I go. Naturally I cannot go back into that same *pharmacia*, so I walk to find another one. Oh yes, the next one knows me, and he asks, "How is the Contessa?" So I said "Fine" and bought aspirin again, and I look for another one, and in this one there is a young salesgirl, so I have to buy more aspirin.

'Well, finally I came to one *pharmacia* where everything was all right; not much light, and one man without a beard, all alone, dusting something, and while looking at some other things I said, "I want so-and-so," and he said, "Small, medium, or large?" and my face got red—how are you supposed to know that?

'Well, I said, "Small, of course," and then I bought other things to make a big package, because when you wrap it up alone, everybody knows what's in it, and then I bought the *Osservatore Romano* and put it around the whole thing. Never again. It took me three hours. We were late for dinner. We are always late.'

The count had succeeded in changing the atmosphere. Charles's face was the happy plum again. He chuckled and asked for cigars, although it was against the rules to smoke cigars in any of these rooms.

The butler passed them with disapproval in his face and movements. The game of do-you-know-so-and-so started, and since the society of Italy, England, and France is extremely mobile and interlarded with Americans, there were many names that everyone knew. Soon they came to the name of a young man of Roman society. 'Yes, I know,' the count said sadly, 'we have many of them.'

'Oh, in that,' said Charles, 'we lead, I'm afraid. Let me tell you what happened to me. One of my best friends was in the same school, served in the same regiment with me, and now, poor chap, can't even visit England. You know who I mean. Everybody knows about it. Lord Peacham.

'Last time I saw him I was with Duff. We were at—what's the name, the hotel in Cairo, Pyramids?—no, something like Semaphor, Semiramis—that's it, the Semiramis. We were in the bar and he was at the other end. Duff recognized him first. Now you can't ignore a chap like Peacham, who's gone to school with you and all that, scandal or no scandal, so we decided that we wouldn't see him while we were drinking, but on the way out we'd pass him and suddenly see him, and say a few words to him. He was near the door, and we decided to shake hands with him there. He was known as Willwill in the old days—Willy's his first name, you know—well, we had decided to do this, and ask after his well-being and so on, so we approach and recognize him, and a frightening thing happens. Willwill stands up and extends his hand, but on to his hand, by way of a wristband, a thin golden chain is attached, and on the other end of this chain—imagine if you can—was a young man, who smiled, and Lord Peacham had the effrontery to introduce him. Well, I might say we left rather hurriedly. The young man giggled.

'Well, there was Lady Peacham, poor darling, she was quite advanced when all this happened, over seventy—well, *he* was around that age at any rate. I saw her in London, and, poor dear, she said to me, "I wish somebody would explain to me why poor Willwill must travel continually"—she said this very sadly—"and why he can't be here where he belongs." Well, I thought that it was high time that someone took the bull by the horns and explained things to her, and I thought the proper person to do that was her brother. I failed to take into account that he was a gruff sort and always had shown a strong dislike for Willwill. But he said he would try and explain things to her, poor darling, and I'm afraid he didn't do any good at all, for Elsie and I visited in England again later and we enquired after Willwill, and Lady Peacham, who is very hard of hearing, said that she was more bewildered than ever. "Imagine," she said, "Derek came to me and said that Willwill had to stay away because he was a bugler."'

'Hahaha, haha, haha,' went the Empty Stomach and proceeded to tell several vulgar and unfunny stories.

The mood was otherwise than it had ever been when Elsie was present.

The Italian countess came in and said that the princess had left and begged to be excused. The count said good night and left with his wife. On the way out they stopped to talk to the wife of the Empty Stomach.

The Empty Stomach stood with Charles and put his hand on Charles's shoulder, and he said, 'You don't like it here,

I know, you're just staying on account of Elsie. Well, I don't like it either, but the Missus likes it here, and she wants to live here, and she has an idea.'

'Yes, she's told me,' said Charles.

'About the house?'

'No, not about the house.'

'Well, this is it in brief. One of these days you won't want this house any more, you know what I mean. Well, you can have it, live in it rent free, until you don't need it any more, and that may be soon, and I buy it from Elsie on that condition. I'll pay her in cash. Let me know the price. Think about it. Good night, Charles. We had a lovely evening.'

He went out with his wife. The servants were putting out the lights. The departing guests were still in the hall.

When the motors started and the doors were closed Mother came down the stairs. She was in turban and robe, and she lay down on the divan.

'I'm sorry about tonight, Elsie dear,' said Charles.

Mother didn't say anything.

Charles said, 'It's late, Elsie.'

She said, 'I have no sense of time any more. I don't know if it's summer, autumn, or winter.'

West came with a thermometer, took the temperature, and said to me, 'Can you read it? I've forgotten my glasses.'

I had glasses, but the room was dark, and Mother said, 'Well, hurry before it goes down to zero. It can't be much.' She turned her head. 'Charles, would you be a dear and light the candles?'

It sounded not at all like her.

Charles searched in his pocket. 'I'm sorry, but I can't find my matches.'

Mother sat up and said in the deep voice and with the bad queen face, 'You don't want a match, Charles, you want a footman. There's the bellcord—pull on it.'

24

Dog Story

Mother was on the terrace. The high glass windows were rolled back. She sat in a very trim metal wheelchair, with the turban on her head, and she looked pale. She was dictating letters to West. At the same time the butler and the young footman were manipulating the gadgets for the eye exercises, and it looked like a large mobile in motion. The servant on the left swung the ping-pong paddle with the black dots like a pendulum, the one on the right went forward and back with a white ball on a stick, and Mother looked here and there to exercise her eyes.

'Good morning,' she said to me and stopped the exercises. 'How do you feel?'

'I feel fine.'

'Well, Mother feels fine, but tomorrow Mother will feel even better, for tomorrow comes a wonderful man, Mr Lasker—let me tell you about him and how Mother got some wonderful medicine that will make her like a little girl again. What is it called, West?'

'It's called cortisone.'

'Well, this dear Mr Lasker is a very rich man, and when he heard how poor Mother felt—I'm not going to bore you with details, we never speak of that, Mother is just telling you a story—well, when he heard how Mother was, he said there was only one thing that would help her, and that was cortisone. Mr Lasker, who is a very intelligent man, besides being a very rich one, has given five million or billion dollars to a hospital in Chicago or in Boston, I don't know, wherever they make cortisone. It's made from something that makes the bulls what they are, and it takes hundreds of thousands of them and it's very expensive—it costs how much, West?'

'Enough for the complete treatment costs around eighteen thousand dollars.'

'Well, Mother loves life and her lovely rooms and Versailles. But she wouldn't put eighteen thousand into this old carcass for anything. She'd rather leave that amount to the little children that she has adopted. So do you know what that kind Mr Lasker did? He said, "Dear Lady Mendl, I wouldn't dream of having you pay for that what's—its—name—cortisone—I shall have it flown over as a gift from me to you." Now, that's what I call friendship, and here comes Dr Lasseur with his needle to give me a shot of friendship.' She put on the little girl wistful smile and raised her gloved hand in salute.

The chauffeur had come in with the doctor, and he wheeled Mother to the foot of the stairs and then carried her upstairs. The doctor followed.

A neighbour, a very severely dressed woman, came to call, and asked how Mother was, and West said that she was well and that in a moment she would receive the visitor.

The neighbour complained about prices.

'You don't have to tell me, just look at this,' said West. 'Read this letter of bitter complaint that Lady Mendl just dictated. Do you see that little bit of new lawn out in front here? It's no bigger than an ordinary living-room carpet. Well, here's the bill for it, and, calculated even at the black-market rate, it comes to five hundred and forty dollars. Well, that's rather high for a piece of grass that wouldn't support even one cow.'

'Life in Paris is awfully dear. But tell me, how is she?' asked the neighbour. 'All the visitors I see coming out of here now wear faces that are already in mourning.'

'How is she? Well, if I didn't have my puthy cats and kitty cats, so that once in a while I'd be with something that knows how to relax, I don't know what I would do. Lady Mendl is a human dynamo going at full speed.'

'But she doesn't look at all well, poor dear.'

'Oh, you should have seen her in Hollywood. She had an operation, she had the highest fever on record and penicillin every hour. You know what she did? She redecorated the floor we were on in that hospital while she was there. In New York she had a heart attack, and we all thought it would be over, and she argued with the doctor. She didn't want to take a boat, she wanted to fly, only at the last minute, because the Line gave us virtually free passage, did she agree to take a boat. On that boat she turned everything upside down. Dr Hauser almost had a nervous breakdown.'

'And dear Sir Charles seems sort of strange. I pass him regularly on the street and there's no sign of recognition.'

Just then there was a signal from upstairs.

'You can go up now.'

'Who was that, West, that went up to see Elsie? She looked familiar. Anybody I know?'

'Of course you know her. It's Lady Renfrew.'

'Louise? Why, I've known her all my life. That was Louise?'

'Yes, that was she. You're not the only one who doesn't recognize her, Sir Charles. She walks up to people at Maxim's who've also known her all her life, and they stare at her and wonder who she is, and only after she speaks do they smile and recognize her. That's what she's done with her face—it's completely new.'

'Who did it?'

'Oh, Franzman—they say he's the best. And there is also the Bogomolets. It kills some people, and others it helps a great deal. It did wonders for her. And there is a real and a fake Bogomolets, they say. The real, black-market Bogomolets comes from Russia. It's something they take from somebody freshly dead; the one you get here is not so good, they say, on account of the time it takes between the accident and the hospital. When you look closely at her, you see all the cuts. I can't understand why they do it. It costs money, it takes time, it's painful, and it doesn't fool anyone. It's much worse than wrinkles. They look like broken masks, and they tell you they feel ten years younger. Why don't they say that they've been in an automobile accident and got cut up? Or why don't they leave themselves alone and grow a nice double chin like me and look like human beings?

'Thank God for my puthy cats and kitty cats. If I didn't have them, I'd have nothing at all in this life! You know, my position in this house has always been difficult. I'm not a servant and I'm not an equal. Many people put their arms around me and don't mean it, and many treat me distantly and don't mean it either. When I am free, what do you think I should do? Where and how shall I live? I'll soon have to think about that.'

'We'll all have to think about it,' said Charles. 'I don't at all like the way she looks.' Charles was sad again, and he put his hand on West's arm.

The doctor came down the stairs, and Charles said to him, 'Tell me frankly, between ourselves, how ill do you yourself really think she is?'

The doctor said, 'Now you have asked me the most difficult question of my whole life. I have never met anyone like her. I can't tell you. She's unlike any woman I've ever known. She lives by her spirit alone, and that spirit is the most formidable, I think, in existence. It may happen in her sleep, at any time now, tonight, when she relaxes. It may not happen for weeks, months, even years. I can't answer your question, Sir Charles, for I am bewildered myself. In fact, it is I who feel ill. She's very well, considering everything.'

There was another signal from upstairs, and West called to the chauffeur, 'Lady Mendl wants to be carried down again. Sorry, Achille.'

'Well, I'm glad she's not Elsa Maxwell,' said the chauffeur.

Charles, who was seated in a corner and invisible to the chauffeur, said sharply, 'Of whom are you speaking, Achille?'

'I beg your pardon, sir,' said Achille. 'I didn't know you was here, sir. I was speaking of Lady Mendl, sir.'

'You see what I mean,' said the doctor, picking up his hat. 'Any other patient would be asleep now, with what I have given her. She wants to go out, and we might as well let her do what she wants. She'll do it anyway.'

'All the same, I don't like it,' said Charles.

The chauffeur was carrying Mother down.

'Come, Stevie, Mother wants to show you something. I have a set of plans in the library, the new designs for the entrance hall. I don't like that place at all the way it is.'

I looked at the sketches of four heroically proportioned panels for the entrance hall. Elsie discussed details with La Flèche, and I went back to Charles.

'I'm not only worried about Elsie, but I'm also worried about money,' he said. 'You know she never thinks of it. West tells me she put some pearls up for sale. These pearls at one time were worth something, but now the pound is bad and pearls are bad. Artificial pearls are so well made they have driven down the price of the good ones. So she is about to sell them for a fraction of their value, and even so it doesn't do any good, it's a drop in the bucket. She had an illusion that everything in France is cheap. Well, it was at one time. When I was at the Embassy before, I bought the wine at diplomats' prices, I got the very best vintages of the very best kinds at less than a dollar a bottle. Now you pay more for it here than you do in America. You know I told her all that in Hollywood, but Elsie doesn't listen to anything that isn't pleasant. Here she comes.'

Elsie said, 'I'm going to change, and then we'll drive to a house in which there is an apartment with the most beautiful *boiseries*—priceless. I looked at them years ago; they weren't for sale then, but now they are. You're coming with me, Stevie. Now, don't go away, I'll be back.' She went up the stairs again in Achille's arms, waving gaily.

West came down after a while and said, 'She's suddenly fallen asleep. She looks like a little tiny bird.'

'Well, send the car away. I'm not going anywhere. I must stay near her.' Charles looked out into the garden.

Mother, on that fateful day, had lunch in bed, and after she came down she sat next to me on the sofa. She smiled and knocked on the floor with the heels of the little girl shoes, and she kicked me in the ribs, but it wasn't the old kind of a kick.

Tea was served. As she poured the milk she said, 'Has Mother told you about Mademoiselle Blanchard?' She smiled the small, furious smile that goes with pain, in which she suddenly showed all her teeth. In between she made faces, mostly grim. She sat quietly for a moment, then said, 'We drove down the Rue Cambon some time ago, the street in back of the Ritz. Well, we got stalled in traffic. We stayed in one place for ten minutes and then moved three feet. I was looking out of the car, and there in the window of a house sat a dog, Stevie, the most beautiful dog—'

Charles interrupted, 'Cat, Elsie dear.'

'Oh yes, cat, the most beautiful cat I ever saw. Well, you know how very fond West is of dogs—'

Charles, with a trace of annoyance, said, 'Cats, Elsie dear.'

Elsie gave him a hard look. 'All right, Charles, cats. Anyway, it was a beautiful grey and white cat. She sat there and we sat there, and the car hadn't moved an inch all this time. So West got out of the car and went to the window, which was open, and said, "Oh, what a lovely puthy cat"—you know the way she talks with cats—and picked it up. The cat belonged to the concièrge, who came crying, and you know how the French can cry. "Oh, please," she cried, "don't do that to my poor cat! Don't touch it! My poor cat has a hernia." I said, "A what?" "A hernia," said the woman. We were still stuck in traffic, and Achille left the wheel and got out, and so did Mother, and Mother said, "Why don't you do something about that poor cat?" So the woman said, "Oh madame, you know one has no money, and it costs so much, everything, and life itself so dear. I am an old woman and I have not enough for myself," and so on. So Mother said to West, "We must do something about that poor dog."'

Charles said, 'Cat,' but Mother paid no attention and continued, 'Well, we took care of the poor cat's operation.' At this stage of the story Mother looked up to the ceiling and smiled sweetly and said in a high voice, 'We certainly took care of that poor cat. She went to a proper dog and cat hospital for a week, and it wasn't a hernia at all.'

Mother folded her hands as in prayer and smiled. 'Well, after a week she came back, and I'm happy to say she's all right now, and we've sent a little milk every day. Achille stops there when he drives me to the hairdresser and leaves a little milk for the puppies.'

'You see, dear boy,' said Charles later, 'that's what worries me. Elsie is getting gaga; now she can't keep dogs and cats apart, and soon the day will come when she won't be able to hold herself together any longer. About that cat whose name is Mademoiselle Blanchard. Hauser had to get pills for her, she was so low, and every day Achille had to take her what was left of the milk from Elsie's breakfast tea and deliver it in the Rue Cambon. With black-market petrol at the price it is, you know, that's being really kind, especially when you hate cats, as Elsie does. But then she thought it was a dog half the time—very confusing that. I'm really worried.'

25

---·---

Aboard the Future

Years ago in New York I saw *Cyrano de Bergerac* with Walter Hampden playing the title role. That production was graced by a most dramatic scene in which Cyrano dies, beautifully sad and autumnal, with golden leaves slowly turning as they sank to the ground. It was a day such as that, the same scene, and the same mood.

Mother sat with the turban on her head, and she was quiet, with her hands folded. It was morning, but she was too tired to do her eye exercises. She was in a dark Mainbocher dress with the small golden fob. Her white-gloved hand came up very slowly to her ear; she indicated that whatever La Flèche had to say he should say it loudly, for he had just been mumbling.

Monsieur La Flèche was measuring a wall. His assistant stood far away from him, holding the other end of a long tape measure.

He shouted, 'Twenty-three metres. What this wants is really one all-over *tapisserie*. There is something that the Louvre is trying to buy. It's in the hands of an antiquarian, and it would fit perfectly here. It is silver and blue, and part of the legend of the daughters of Danaüs. We could look at it. It belonged to a set woven for Louis Fifteenth.'

'Make an appointment,' said Mother.

Monsieur La Flèche wrote down the measurements in his book and left.

Mother touched my arm and smiled weakly. 'Something very nice happened to Mother yesterday. There's something wonderful about having good friends. Now Paul Louis Weiller is a good friend. You know what he did? He came and said that someone had told him that I wanted to sell my pearls, and he asked could he have a look at them. So I had them brought down, and he said he loved them, and he paid me more than I had paid for them. Stevie, that is friendship.

'Now, stay with me, for the little children are coming. I gave orders right after they came that no one was to be allowed to see them and that they were to be left alone, so they won't get the idea that they're on exhibition or that they have to love me. Well, the experiment worked out wonderfully. They are all of them talented, it seems—even the little coloured baby has got the hang of things and sings beautifully. They are coming over, and you must stay with Mother and see what they have done, for they are bringing their first work with them.'

They came in new outfits, all dressed as individuals, and they had changed into a group of ordinary children. Mother asked them to come forward one at a time, and she said to each in turn, 'What is it you want to be when you grow up?'

The first little boy looked at her and said, 'I want to be a composer like my papa.'

'Very well, you shall be one. And you, Micheline?'

'I want to be a dress designer.'

'Bravo!'

'And you, little Armand?'

'I want to be a painter.'

'Show milady what you have done,' said the English nanny who had replaced the Frenchwoman.

The children crowded forward, and each held high in his hand a painting, a sheet of music, a doll dressed in clothes made by its *'maman'*, architectural designs, watercolours, and models of things. All of them had been made with earnest endeavour, and the things that were visual had spirit and were done with talent.

The composer ran on his little legs to the piano and played a short piece. One who wanted to be a writer recited something. At last little Jones was presented. He had taken in the entire scene; his intelligent face had turned to wherever something was happening, and he seemed to record it all in his young brain—sound, smell, and form. He looked as if he wanted to comment, but words were not at his command, and so he made elaborate sounds of happiness; perhaps they should have given him a drum to beat.

The nurse came forward and said, 'Would you mind very much if they kissed you, Lady Mendl?'

'Not at all,' said Mother. They came up to her and kissed her as one does a religious statue.

The mood of things Spanish, of death, religion, and incense, was in the room again, as it had been on the first day I met her.

There were two more children, the sister and brother who had stood close together the first day I saw them at the kindergarten. They still were hand in hand, and as yet had not spoken. They were still thin and serious, and as *sage* as only

French children can look. They approached, and Elsie took
them in her arms, and then, holding each by one hand, she
asked them what they wanted to be. The little girl said she
wanted to be an interior decorator; the boy said he wanted to
be an architect and to build beautiful things. 'We could like
that very much if it were possible,' they said.

For a moment Mother's mouth went out of control; it trem-
bled, and her eyes watered. But then she clamped her lips tight
and made the Voltaire face; she swallowed and said, 'You shall
be a decorator, my darling, you shall be the very best, I see it
in you. And you shall be an architect. All of you shall be what
you want to be.

'Come closer to me, my children. Stand here where I can
touch you.' They all crowded around her. Mother spoke slowly.
'I suppose you young people know that you belong to the only
aristocracy left on earth, the aristocracy of the arts and profes-
sions. You breathe the rarefied atmosphere of the only people
whose work and achievements endure.

'Everything comes and goes—kings, queens, dictators,
millionaires—but only the artist remains. Because art is beauty,
and beauty, as a poet once said, is truth, and that is all you know
on earth, and all you need to know.

'And so all I can say to you young people, for your future, is:
Just you stay real "pros" and nothing can ever happen to you.'

They understood. They took their leave very elegantly.
Little Jones looked most gravely over the shoulder of the nurse.
And when they were gone Mother cried, as the French say,
like a fountain.

She excused herself and said, 'You know, I think this is the
first time in my life that I have wept. I had difficulty talking to

them, I could hardly speak, and I had to, especially to that little girl, the last one, who wants to be a decorator. I saw that there I myself stood again. You know, her name is Elisabeth la Cloche. We'll change that to Elsie—I can see it written on a little shop window in the Place Vendôme. I've seen my lawyer, and every one of them is taken care of. I've provided for their education, and they all have a fund for travel and a little something to start them off with a shop or an atelier.' Mother dried her eyes.

Charles, who was sitting with us, looked at her worriedly, for all the danger signals were there.

'It's black, Stevie. It's all in deepest black, as for mourning,' said Mother.

West said, 'Lady Mendl is speaking of the accountant's statements. She's afraid she will die poor or have to give up the villa and move to a hotel.'

'In that case I would prefer to die here,' said Elsie. 'You know, one can order death, the way one orders breakfast in a good hotel. I feel I shall order it soon.'

A moment later she was resolute again, and the Voltaire face appeared, and a kick in my ribs, but not the kind that let you know she meant what she said.

She ordered cards, and the butler came with a letter on his tray.

West was about to give her empty teacup to the butler, when she looked into it and said, 'Oh, you know, Lady Mendl, what I see here? I see a large man approaching this house—and he is very rich. He's carrying two heavy bags of money—just look, it's clear as anything.'

'Well, we shall welcome him with open arms,' said Mother, looking into the cup. 'Do you believe in omens, Charles?'

'Rot and nonsense.'

The card table was in place and the glass elephant waiting.

'I have an apology to make,' said Charles, shuffling the cards.

'What about?'

'About the Empty Stomach, my dear. I'm afraid you were right about him.'

'What's wrong with him?'

'Oh, he's gross and awful and utterly without any manners—I mean, one doesn't expect them of him, but people like that sometimes have a kind of manners of the heart.'

'Why, what's he done?'

'I don't know whether or not I should tell you this. Well, to begin with, his wife made me a proposition that is too disgusting even to repeat, and then he came and made me a proposition also.'

'And was that less disgusting, Charles?'

'It wasn't disgusting, it was merely crude.'

'Well, what was it?'

'He offered to buy this house—' Charles hesitated.

'Yes, go on.'

'He offered to buy this house—after—'

'After I am dead.'

'Yes, after that, Elsie.'

'Well, did he say what he'd pay for it?'

'Oh, the price seems no object, dear.'

'But what's all the fuss about then?'

'He wants to buy it now.'

'Yes, but I'm not dead yet.'

'That's just it, Elsie, he wants you—that is, he wants us—to live here, and then eventually he will take the house.'

'After I'm gone.'

'That's right, dear.'

Elsie thought for a while and made all her faces, from Voltaire to little girl, and finally she said, 'But that's a very nice idea, Charles.'

'Do you think so, dear?'

'He's rich, isn't he?'

'Yes, very rich, one of the richest men in the world.'

'Well, Charles, put down those cards and get to him before he changes his mind. Get him and have the sales contract drawn up. Get him right away. Go talk to him on the phone immediately.'

Mother was her old self again. She called West and gave a dozen orders. Everything was arranged with the Empty Stomach. The price for the villa was to be paid in the usual complicated fashion of such deals, so much in francs, declared for tax purposes in France, and so much in New York. Mother was an expert on all these matters.

It took some time to agree on a price and to draw up the papers, and then an appointment was made with the Empty Stomach and his lawyer, and Mother also thought it would be good to have present the clerk of the commune of Versailles, if not the mayor, so that the instrument would be properly notarized.

On the day of the meeting, which was set for ten a.m., a long table was placed in the salon. It was covered with billiard cloth, there were blotters and inkstands and new pens in pen-holders.

At precisely ten that morning the notary of the commune of Versailles was there, wearing his sash, without which no act of his is official.

Mother sat on the divan, her second-best fur blanket over her legs. For the first time she wore no gloves. She looked her age. She wore a grey gauze turban and no jewels. Her lawyer was next to her.

Charles walked up and down outside, on the terrace. Then the butler announced the car. The Empty Stomach came in with a secretary and his lawyer; they were all very grave. After elaborate greetings everybody sat down at the table, and Achille, who had lifted Mother into her wheelchair, rolled her to the head of the table, to a place between the Empty Stomach and his lawyer. Mother was given the contract to read, and she went over it very carefully. It was agony to watch her. Her hands were completely dead. The veins lay atop the hands as they do in anatomic models for students to learn where the blood vessels are. She looked up at the Empty Stomach, and she opened her mouth and closed her eyes. She lay back as if she were fainting away, and she said, 'It seems all right to me.'

One of the lawyers put a pen into Elsie's trembling hand. She again took a while before she spoke, and then motioned to the Empty Stomach to come closer. As if with the last breath she would draw, looking at the Empty Stomach, as if she couldn't clearly see him, she said in a hoarse whisper, 'I hope that you love houses as I do.'

'Yes, I do, Lady Mendl.'

'I wonder if you would do me a small favour.'

'Certainly, anything, Lady Mendl,' said the Empty Stomach.

'We must do this properly, Mr Munchin. Could we insert a little clause somewhere in here, something to the effect that I may make some badly needed repairs and improvements in this place? You see, it's a historic monument and an old, old house. It has suffered a lot. It was occupied first by the Germans, then by the Americans, and after that by the French, and I want you to get this house in decent shape. So, in other words, I'll really be decorating it for you, without charging you a penny for my services.' This speech took a long time, for there were many pauses.

Mother leaned back, exhausted. The Empty Stomach looked at his lawyer, and the lawyer took one look at Mother and then looked back at his client and nodded.

'I'll dictate it, if you don't mind, and then we'll sign the agreement,' Mother said weakly.

While she dictated to her lawyer the Empty Stomach got up and looked around with proprietary interest. 'Well,' he said, 'we're lucky to have the benefit of Lady Mendl's taste. She'll put the place in shape.' He held his hand flat against the strip of antique wood where the french doors closed, to see if any air leaked in, and he looked at the floor and at the light brackets that might need a little fixing.

'See if that's in order with you,' said Mother, handing the paper to the lawyer of the Empty Stomach.

The lawyer read it, with his index finger moving along the words. He nodded as he read.

While the lawyer read, Mother spoke again to Mr Munchin. 'There's one more thing.'

'Yes, Lady Mendl.'

'You're going to leave everything as it is, aren't you?'

'Exactly as it is, Lady Mendl,' said the Empty Stomach.

Mother closed her eyes and put her hand on her heart. 'I'm sorry to be so much trouble, Mr Munchin, but would you mind putting a little rider into that contract?'

'It depends what it's about,' he said.

Elsie looked at Mr Munchin, and he and his lawyer moved closer, for it was almost impossible to understand what she was saying. She raised her voice with tremendous effort. 'I would like to have a clause put in to the effect that I may buy back the place at what you are paying for it, plus the cost of the improvements, plus a reasonable interest, any time within the next ten years.'

The Empty Stomach did not bother to consult his attorney. He said emphatically, 'Certainly, Lady Mendl, and I waive any interest.'

The lawyer nodded benevolently, for it seemed as if Mother was sinking away and these were her last words.

'Well, now, put that in writing, and let's initial it, and have the whole thing witnessed and notarized so that it is all simple, clear, and airtight.'

This took a while. The butlers came and served champagne. After everything was legalized the notary of the commune of Versailles performed his rites and packed away his stamps and his gold and blue sash. The goodbyes were said. The cheque which the Empty Stomach had written was in the hands of Elsie's lawyer.

The sand in the roadway crunched under the wheels of the departing cars. Eugénie brought down a new pair of white gloves, and a magnificent Schiaparelli shawl, for Mother had said that she was cold. Suddenly, as she pulled the gloves on, her voice changed. In parade-ground tones she boomed, 'Has he gone?'

'Yes, he's gone,' said Monsieur La Flèche. He came into the room with his assistants, two young men who carried saw-boards, sawhorses, and rolls of plans.

'Now we'll start to work,' said Mother. 'Where is West?'

The second man looked for West.

'Ah, *la joie de vivre*,' said West. 'Here we go again. Tell Lady Mendl I'll be there in a second. I have to see my kitty cats and puthy cats first, before I can face what's coming.'

When she returned, Mother, who was young again, said, 'West, first of all get ahold of What's-his-name, who has the tapestry for this wall. Tell him it's bought; then we shall see about the *boiseries*. And that measly piece of lawn out there—West, tell Fleurtry to call the grass people. I want the whole park out there one green, green carpet from here to the horizon. Oh, this is all so wonderful! I won't be able to sleep a wink tonight.

'Stevie, sit down here next to Mother. Now look across the garden, and there to the right you see a reflecting pool, and in it a little temple of love, with a statue, and in back of that a wall of pink terracotta against which the white rambler roses grow. The way you see it now, it's all cock-eyed. When Mother bought this place the ground to the left was not to be had for love or money—now it is for sale. So Mother is going to buy it, and then we'll move the reflecting pool and the temple and the wall over, so that they are properly centred and the eye has something to rest on besides the horizon, for any farm has that.

'Now, isn't it wonderful, Stevie, to have friends? To have good friends, that is the most important thing in life,' said Mother and gave me a kick in the ribs that had the old force to it.

Monsieur La Flèche had unrolled his plans on the green table, and suddenly nothing outside them existed any more for Mother.

I walked into the lobby. Charles was standing there, in homburg hat, as Coombs helped him into his coat. He pulled on his gloves, took his cane, and marched towards the door.

'I feel a great deal better,' he said in the Foreign Office tone. 'For now dear Elsie's going to live forever.'

POSTSCRIPT

———•———

I have designed a few characters that do not resemble anyone in real life but are aggregates of various people. For example, the Empty Stomach and Mrs Munchin are invented; they represent the phantoms Elsie fought, the enemies of her perfect Eden, rather than actual persons living. It wasn't the Empty Stomach who bought the house but her good friend Paul Louis Weiller, who had extended help and friendship to her. Naturally, the servants also are fictitious.

I have drawn Lady Mendl exactly as she appeared to me, and does today, for I think of her often and I shall miss her always.

For the rest, I have availed myself of the devices of fiction to bridge places and time. The bathroom, for example, that I placed in Beverly Hills was really in Lady Mendl's house at Number 10, Avenue d'Iéna, Paris. Otherwise the scene is much as it was.

L.B.
Paris, 1954

Hotel Splendide

Ludwig Bemelmans

———•———

Welcome to the grand Hotel Splendide in nineteen twenties
New York, where hilarity and chaos reign. In the mirror-
lined dining halls, the champagne is constantly flowing; in
the kitchens downstairs, malcontent waiters incite revolution.

In this classic memoir, Ludwig Bemelmans encounters
eccentricity on every level of the hotel hierarchy as he
works his way up from busboy at the restaurant's most
undesirable table, to assistant manager of the magnificent
private banquets. There may be Russian ballerinas
and Wall Street tycoons to entertain, but there is also
Mespoulets, the world's worst waiter, to contend with and
a murder plot against Monsieur Victor, the authoritarian
maître d'hôtel, to solve. Accompanied by Bemelmans'
own witty illustrations, this account of a bygone era of
extravagance is as charming as it is riotously entertaining.

AVAILABLE AND COMING SOON
FROM PUSHKIN PRESS

Pushkin Press was founded in 1997, and publishes novels, essays, memoirs, children's books—everything from timeless classics to the urgent and contemporary.

Our books represent exciting, high-quality writing from around the world: we publish some of the twentieth century's most widely acclaimed, brilliant authors such as Stefan Zweig, Yasushi Inoue, Teffi, Antal Szerb, Gerard Reve and Elsa Morante, as well as compelling and award-winning contemporary writers, including Dorthe Nors, Edith Pearlman, Perumal Murugan, Ayelet Gundar-Goshen and Chigozie Obioma.

Pushkin Press publishes the world's best stories, to be read and read again. To discover more, visit www.pushkinpress.com.

THE PASSENGER
ULRICH ALEXANDER BOSCHWITZ

AT NIGHT ALL BLOOD IS BLACK
DAVID DIOP

TENDER IS THE FLESH
AGUSTINA BAZTERRICA

WHEN WE CEASE TO UNDERSTAND THE WORLD
BENJAMÍN LABATUT

THE WONDERS
ELENA MEDEL

NO PLACE TO LAY ONE'S HEAD
FRANÇOISE FRENKEL